POWER
Marketing
YOUR NOVEL

ISBN 1-881164-88-8

1st Printing: 2000

Cover: Raul Melendez
Typography: Monica S. Rozier

Library of Congress Cataloguing -in-Publication Data

Spizer, Joyce.
  Power marketing your novel: marketing and promoting
  fiction and nonfiction / by Joyce Spizer
      p.   cm.
  Includes bibliographical references and index.
  ISBN 1-881164-88-8
      1. Fiction – Authorship – Marketing.   I. Title.

PN3365 .S68 2000
808.3– dc21
                                                    00-029566

POWER

Marketing
YOUR NOVEL
**Marketing and Promoting
Fiction and Nonfiction**

by
Joyce Spizer

INTERCONTINENTAL PUBLISHING

Acknowledgments:

A special thanks to Doris Elaine Fell, author of *The Sagas of Kindred Heart Series*. She's been my friend, a profound teacher, an inspiration, and official editor throughout my writing career. Her bubbly laughter and dry wit, accompanied by her sharp edit marks, keep me alert and on-point. I get away with nothing.

To *Daisey Trotman*, my redheaded associate and dear friend, whose rich southern accent and boundless energy kept my office and my life going during the final deadline hours for this book. She may think her job is done. Have I told her I'm writing five more?

To Carolyn Reynolds, friend, astrologer, and author (*The Book of Lovers*), whose role in my life changes daily. When I first met this beautiful redheaded lady, she read my astrological chart. She interpreted my future in the field of writing expanding into a new area. Maybe I'm a teacher.

To *Patrick Hartley*, Carolyn's husband, who took time from his busy schedule to take my husband, Harold, golfing so I could complete two books and Carolyn could work on hers. We are blessed to have such understanding fellows.

To Jane Guttman, D.C., who found my article in *The Desert Woman* and called me for marketing advice. The synchronicity of our lives during her personal search and the debut of her nonfiction novel, *The Gift Wrapped in Sorrow*, is not mere chance. Her warm spirit and healing powers simply cannot be ignored. I am blessed.

And for all the aspiring writers in the world who envision a day when a truck will come to your home and off-load boxes filled with dreams—your book in your arms, at last. I applaud your commitment to your story, your dedicated hard work and unending enthusiasm. May you all have best sellers.

This book is dedicated to my loving husband,
Harold Spizer,
who introduced me to the more practical
concepts of marketing and promotion.
There are extraordinary challenges
in everyday life, in relationships, and
in the business world.
For the author it's the struggle for
sales and recognition.
And he inspired me to share
these visions with you.

Do you know,
Considering the market, there are more
Poems produced than any other thing?
No wonder poets sometimes have to seem
So much more businesslike than businessmen.
Their wares are so much harder to get rid of.
Robert Frost, *New Hampshire,* 1923

Disclaimer

As with any publication that contains names, addresses, telephone numbers, FAX numbers and Internet information, you must always investigate its accuracy. This world moves on wheels and the only constant in this life is change.

Although the author exhaustively researched all sources to ensure the accuracy and completeness of the information contained herein, she assumes no responsibility for errors, inaccuracies, omissions, or any other inconsistency herein. People move, businesses close, philosophies change. That's life. Any perceived slights against people or organizations are unintentional.

The author does not endorse, recommend, or support any sources listed herein, nor can she validate their competence, or credibility. Readers should consult their loved ones, or accountant, publicist, agent, editor, or other outside sources, and their own good judgement before engaging in, supporting, or funding any ventures suggested in this book.

POWER Marketing YOUR NOVEL

Table of Contents

1. It's Never Too Early to Plan

- A business plan
- The marketing plan
- Book awards
- Set a realistic promotional budget
- Establishing a promotional time-line
- Getting those all-important reviews

2. "Heavens! How Can I Ever Give a Speech?"

- Be prepared
- Speak with enthusiasm and warmth
- The early bird gets the book sales
- "Speak the speech I pray you . . ."
- Savor the applause; sell those books
- What makes a speech successful?

3. It's Tool Time!

- Business cards
- Private box number
- Telephones
- 1-800 or 1-888 numbers

- Press kits and photos
- Letterheads and envelopes for your stationery
- Zip code book and postal scales
- Bulk mail
- Shipping boxes and large envelopes
- Calendars
- Computer and printer
- Fax machine
- Label maker
- Goodies: T-shirts, mugs, tote bags, etc.
- Flyers and brochures
- Access to a central library
- Credit cards
- Web site
- E-mail

4. Get organized
- Networking
- Obtain mailing lists
- Educate yourself
- Attend conferences
- Join speaker bureaus
- Develop resources

5. Who, when and how to "book 'em"
- What about the tour?
- How do you find bookings?
- Non-traditional markets
- Reducing your costs
- Creating your publicity package
- Press releases
- Clipping services

6. Whose publicists are they anyway?

- How do you find them?
- What are your goals?
- What do you want them to do?
- Can you afford it?
- What can you do yourself?

7. Dress to sell

- Packing for the tour
- How do the professionals interview?
- Dressing to be remembered

8. Your business plan—staying alive, staying alive

- How to sustain sales when your fifteen minutes of fame has passed
- Other ideas to consider
- Audio and video packaging
- Value-added products
- Ready for your close up?

9. The inner sanctum of the Internet

- It helps if you have a ten-year old at home who can help you
- Setting up a web site
- Is everybody else out there doing this too? You bet!
- Online interviews, reviews and selling

10. More marketing mania

- There are ten seasons of book selling
- Did you think about this?
- Newsletters
- Sell on television

Introduction

Congratulations! You've written a book. After numerous revisions and many rejections, you've signed a contract with a major house, a small independent press, or maybe you contacted a printer with an eye toward self-publishing.

You may think you can kick back and wait for those royalty checks. Browse *Publishers Weekly* for those glowing reviews. Did *Oprah* call? Or *Leno* and *Letterman* to book you on the late-night talk-show circuit?

Consider this, if you think your participation in this project is over. All those hours writing, proofreading and making changes were infinitesimal components of becoming an author. Who's is going to sell that first edition?

You are!

Hey, wait just a minute, you're thinking. My publisher promised to do all the marketing. They're orchestrating my book tours. They'll handle all the publicity. I'm the author.

Wrong! You're the information system, the conductor who will orchestrate your success and failure as an author. Marketing and promoting is another phase of your work and begins the moment you sign that all-important contract.

From that point on, you become a partner with the publisher, or, if you're self-publishing, the managing director of promotion and marketing.

Where do you begin? If you have *some* concept, or not the vaguest idea: This book has been written with *you* in mind. It represents the best of all writing worlds, covering the processes you should know before launching your book.

During my debut book tour, I made a million mistakes, scored numerous successes and picked up a world of pointers along the way. This guide is filled with those experiences – the good, the bad and the ugly.

You may think your book is the grandest product of all times. A surefire hit. A blockbuster. A classic that will live forever. Good! You've mastered the first step: Believing in your product.

This book will help you with the next step: Attracting buyers for your product.

So, come along with me on tour. Grab that highlighter and let's go to work.

1

It's Never Too Early to Plan

Congratulations, you're an author. You followed all the primary writing rules. Your work appears professional on paper. You read lots of "how-to" books and know everything about the writer's bible, the *Literary Market Place* also known as the *LMP*. You subscribe to and/or diligently read several magazines that have their pulse on the publishing industry: i.e., *Publishers Weekly*, 245 West 17th Street, New York, New York 10011; (212) 463-6758, FAX: (212) 463-6631, and *Writer's Digest*, 1507 Dana Avenue, Cincinnati, Ohio 45207.

You mastered your craft at creative writing classes and worked with a local critique group to make the book the best work it can be. You networked the industry's pulse at writers conferences, joined local, regional, national, and world-wide writing organizations, and told all your friends and family about your novel.

You found an agent and/or publisher and the book's ready to be published. Now head for that dark solitary work room to write the sequel.

Wait a minute. Who's going to sell the first one? Unless you're fortunate enough to be a major celebrity or someone with spontaneous name recognition, have an unlimited budget, and a full-time publicist—you are. Stephen King can phone his publicity in, but you can't.

First, you must establish a depth of knowledge in marketing your genre. That takes a lot of research. It isn't necessary to know everything, but research puts you on the leading edge of expertise. After all, your book will compete with 55,000 to 60,000 others that are published the same year.

Ideally, the business and marketing plans should be developed a year to eighteen months before publication. Two weeks before the book is in your hands is too late to catch the "gold ring."

The success of any book depends on a business and marketing plan, a realistic financial budget, and a book promotion time-line. Remember, a plan is simply that. Flexibility and experimentation are key elements to its success. Some ideas will work for certain authors and genres, other concepts fail miserably. Books, like first-run motion pictures, have short lives, often less than ninety days.

The Business Plan

Answer these basic questions:

- Who will buy my book?
- How do I position myself in the market to guarantee sales?
- How do I create a desire for my work?
- How do I sustain the sales over a period of time?

Of course, your friends and family will buy one. After signing at the local bookstores, who else is there? This book helps you identify the target markets.

Positioning yourself in the market to guarantee sales takes a lot of creativity. It means catching the season if it's a holiday book. If the novel is about mothers and daughters, posture a spring release to coincide with Mother's Day. If the book is about an illness, like kidney disease; contact the National Kidney Foundation. When is their Special Olympics held? When is Organ Donor Month? National Kidney Week? Use your genre, your career, and the book's theme to develop other markets who will sell for you.

HINT: Living in today's publishing environment brings unique challenges. In my small community, four months before speaking to 2,000 women, I approached the manager of a chain store and asked him to order my book. He ordered three copies. Literally, I sold my inventory from the trunk of the car.

A few months later, I approached the store manager again. I was a keynote speaker for another conference that anticipated over four hundred attendees. The manager referred me to their "regional supervisor" with my dilemma. The store ordered three copies.

While the "perennial" authors mean sure sales for bookstores, the mid-list authors struggle. But don't be discouraged. Create your own alternative markets.

I found a small independent book store that has a great location, constant foot traffic, and advertises. I introduced myself to the owner as a local author who needed someone to carry and hand-sell my book. She's sold hundreds to date.

It's a win-win for us both. When I speak, her store is the one I advertise. She receives free advertising and new customers from me. As a bonus, she has autographed first editions on display at the counter and in the genre area. A mid-list publisher or small press book can't buy that counter or book space at the larger stores.

The lesson is: sometimes you have to work outside the box. When you can't accomplish things in a direct way, move outside the box, and develop your own distribution path.

Create a desire for this work by hyping it everywhere you go, to everyone you meet. Develop "sound bytes" that peak curiosity in others. A "sound byte" is the head-turning, gasping, breath-catching hook that grabs the reader's attention.

HINT: The "sound byte" for my debut novel, *The Cop was White as Snow was,* "I saw my first dead body when I was twenty-one years old."

A darling octogenarian told me, "I don't know if I have a story or not. I was...(insert name of powerful Hollywood producer of the 1950's)...mistress for twenty-three *years."*

Make the listener/reader beg for more. Write a freelance article with excerpts. Make an announcement about this work every waking moment. A list of great sources otherwise overlooked are listed throughout this book.

HINT: I'm often asked the question, "How much time do *you* spend marketing?"

"From the time I get up every morning, until the last light is turned out at bedtime," is my answer.

Sell. Sell. Sell.

As the book tour slows down, develop a series of speaking engagements. Attend conferences as a panelist, moderator, or keynote speaker. Join speaker bureaus, develop lecture programs, and teach creative writing.

You are now the expert on your body of work. There are no limitations to the exposure you can receive, when you're positioned correctly in the market.

If your budget allows, and your book's message so unique—advertise in *Radio-TV Interview Report, Spec Marketplace*, and contact all national television talk shows.

- *Radio-TV Interview Report*, Bradley Communications Corporation, 135 East Plumstead Avenue, P. O. Box 1206, Lansdowne, PA 19050-8206. (800) 989-1400, ext. 117. FAX: (610) 284-3704
- *Spec Book Marketplace*, P. O. Box 1356, Santa Monica, CA 90406. (310) 396-1662. They also advertise scripts.

Want to know how to reach *Oprah, Montel, Geraldo, Hard Copy*? For the latest in up-to-date information on booking everything from major network talk shows, regional and local talk shows, and the more obscure media markets you might subscribe to:

- John Kremer's *Book Marketing Updates*. Published

twice a month by Bradley Communications Corporation, 135 East Plumstead Avenue, P. O. Box. 1206, Lansdowne, PA 19050-8206. (800) 989-1400 ext 432, FAX: (610) 284-3704. E-mail: <JohnKremer@bookmarket.com>

The only limitations you face are time, money, and the energy you are willing to expend to make your project successful.

The Marketing Plan

Your marketing plan should be:

- Aggressive—months before the publication date
- Intensive—during launch
- Steady—to keep in the forefront as new books try to bump your product off the shelf

Focus on developing a network of contacts like bookstores and libraries that will vigorously promote your work. Don't overlook resources in cities where you currently live and work, and all others since your birth. Pay particular attention to schools you attended. School mates read, they buy books, and they'll either love or hate the concept that you're successful. Spread the word. Discover conferences that promote mid-list authors and encourage your participation. Maintain a flexible plan and don't be bashful about eliminating ideas that bomb.

During this time, your author *persona* is blossoming. Cultivate your speaking style and "sound bytes." These are critical when greeting potential customers and encouraging them to buy your book. Try, "I'm a guide-dog instructor." Or

6

"My father was a cat-burglar." Think you're trying to sell the first book?

Yes, of course you are. But, in reality you're developing those repeat customers and finding fans who'll carry the message to others. The key to bringing your novel to the attention of the world is networking and finding that special something that culls your book from the herd of average stories. Force readers to take notice.

The time frame from contract—to print—to the public is a major source of frustration and mystery for most authors. Don't let this discourage you. This book is designed to walk you through the learning process.

Book Awards

Book awards are often overlooked by publishing houses and authors alike. The large houses say awards don't sell books, because by the time the awards are given, the shelf life of your book is over at the large chains. It does, however, enhance your value as an author when contracting for future books. For the small and independent presses that keep your book on the shelves longer, awards do matter.

By genre, you will find all the award information, including guidelines, deadlines, and committees listed in magazines, newsletters, the Internet chat clubs, organizations you join, and the all important *Literary Market Place (LMP)*. You may need to nominate the book yourself. Others have—don't be shy. Here are the more popular ones:

- AI of P: The Children's Science Writing Award in Physics and Astronomy awarded by the American Institute of Physics, 500 Sunnyside Blvd, Woodbury,

New York 11797-2999; (516) 576-2200, FAX: (516) 576-2327. E-mail: <info@aip.org> or <http://www.aip.org>

- ALA, also known as the American Library Association, presents the Denali Press Award recognizing the best minority and ethnic reference books. Contact them at 50 E. Huron Street, Chicago, Ill 60611-2795; (800) 545-2433, FAX: (312) 944-8741 Home Page: <http://www.ala.org/editions>

- AMWA Medical Book Awards—The American Medical Writers Association honors physicians, health professionals and all medical writers. Contact them at 9650 Rockville Pike, Bethesda, MD 20814; (301) 493-0003. FAX: (301) 493-6384

- The Advertising Marketing & Sales Promotion Book Club, Book Club Building, Dept LMP, 7 Putter Lane, Middle Island, New York 11953-0102; (516) 924-8555 ext. 100. FAX: (516) 924-3890. E-mail: <linickgrp@att.net> or <http://www.linickgroup.com>

- American Book Awards—known as the ABA Awards for fiction and nonfiction, Before Columbus Foundation, The Raymond House, 655 13th Street, Suite 300, Oakland, CA 94612; (510) 268-9775

- American Booksellers Book of the Year—children and adult novels, 828 South Broadway, Tarrytown, New York 10591; (914) 591-2665 or (800) 637-0037, FAX: (914) 591-2720. E-mail: <preynol@bookweb.org> or <http://www.bookweb>

- Benjamin Franklin Book Awards—small press titles. Publishers Marketing Association, 627 Aviation Way, Manhattan Beach, CA 90266; (310) 372-2732, FAX:

8

(310) 374-3342. E-mail: <pmaonline@aol.com> or <http://www.pma-online.org>

- Best Cookbook of the Year—also known as the James Beard Book Award, contact M. Young Comm, 80 Fifth Avenue, Suite 705, New York, New York 10011; (212) 620-7027, FAX: (212) 645-3654
- Book Show Awards—recognizes book designers and producers. Contact them at Wadsworth Publishing, 10 Davis Drive, Belmont, CA 94002; (650) 595-2350 or (800 354-9706, FAX: (650) 592-3342
- ByLine Literary Awards—offers prizes from more than 50 genres, from limericks to short stories to subscribers of this national magazine. For guidelines contact them at P. O. Box 130596, Edmond, OK 73013
- California Writers Club—six category contest for unpublished material. They're at 2214 Derby Street, Berkeley, CA 94705
- E.C.P.A. Awards—acknowledges 20 Christian book publishers a year. Contact Evangelical Christian Publishers Association, 1969 E. Broadway Road, Suite 2, Tempe, AZ 85282; (602) 966-3998, FAX: (602) 966-1944. E-mail: <dross@ecpa.org> or <http://www.ecpa.org>
- Ernest Hemingway Foundation—presents the Pen Award for First Fiction in literary excellence. Pen American Center, 568 Broadway, Suite 401, New York, New York 10012; (212) 334-1660, FAX: (212) 334-2181. E-mail: <pen@echonyc.com>
- Gold Ink Awards—offers 21 category winners. Publishing and Production Executive, North American Publishing, 401 N. Broad Street, Philadelphia, PA

19108-1074; (215) 238-5300, FAX: (215) 238-5457

- Heartland Prizes—mid-west fiction and nonfiction. Contact Chicago Tribune % Nelson Algren Awards, Literary Awards, 435 North Michigan Avenue, Chicago, Ill 60611-4041
- Hugo and Nebula Awards—science fiction and fantasy is sponsored by the World Science Fiction Society, P. O. Box 1270, Kendall Square Station, Cambridge, MA 02142; (617) 244-2679
- IACP Julia Child Cookbook Awards—honoring the best of food and beverage books. International Association of Culinary Professionals, 304 W. Liberty, Suite 201, Louisville, KY 40202; (502) 581 9786, FAX (502) 589-3602
- James Beard Book Awards—formerly known as the R. T. French Tastemaker Award. For the cooks in your home contact James Beard Foundation, 167 West 12th Street, New York, New York 10011; (212) 675-4984 or 620-7093 or (800) 37-BEARD; FAX: (212) 645-1438. For additional information contact M. Young Comm. 80 Fifth Avenue, Suite 705, New York, New York 10011; (212) 620-7027, FAX: (212) 645-3654
- LMP Awards—has ten annual awards. R. R. Bowker Company, 121 Chanlon Road, New Providence, New Jersey 07974; (908) 464-6800, FAX: (908) 508-7696. E - m a i l : < i n f o @ b o w k e r . c o m > o r <http://www.bowker.com>
- Malcom Cowley Prize—Viking Penguin offers a cash award for an unpublished work of fiction or nonfiction. Contact them at 375 Hudson Street, New York, New York 10014; (212) 366-2000, FAX: (212) 266-2666

- NABE Book of the Year Awards—annual awards for Independent Book Publishers. Contact Al Galasso, President of the North America Bookdealer's Exchange at P. O. Box 606, Cottage Grove, OR 97424; Telephone and FAX: (541) 942-7455. E-mail: <marketbooks@juno.com> or <http://bookmarketingprofits.com>
- NCCJ Mass Media Awards—for the best book on human relations contact the National Conference of Christians and Jews, 71 Fifth Avenue, Suite 1100, New York, New York 10003; (212) 206-0006, FAX: (212) 255-6177
- National Book Critics Circle Book Awards—biography, fiction and nonfiction, and poetry. Contact Art Winslow at The Nation, 72 Fifth Avenue, New York, New York 10011; (516) 454-2020 Home Page: <http://bookwire.com>
- National Jewish Book Awards—recognizes twenty novels each year, JWB, Jewish Book Council, 15 East 26th Street, New York, New York 10010; (212) 532-4949
- Newbery Medal—also known as the John Newbery Medal for children's books is offered by the American Library Association, % The Association for Library Service to Children, 50 East Huron Street, Chicago, Ill 60611-2795; (312) 280-2163 or (800)545-2433, FAX: (312) 280-3257. E-mail: <alsc@ala.org> or <http://www.ala.org/alsc>
- Nobel Prize—for literature sponsored by the Nobel Foundation (Nobelstiftelsen), P. O. Box 5232 (Sturegatan 14) 5-102 45 Stockholm, Sweden,

Telephone 8-663-09-20, FAX: 8-660-38-47. E-mail: <into@nobel.se> or <http://www.nobel.se>

- Ozzie Awards—has 50 categories in the area of design. South Wind Publications, 8340 Mission Road, Suite 106, Prairie Village, KS 66206; (913) 642-6611, FAX: (913) 642-6676
- PIA Graphic Arts Awards—is a design award. Printing Industries of America, 100 Dangerfield Road, Alexandria, VA 22314; (703) 841-8153 or (800) 315-9149, FAX: (703) 548-3227 <www.printinc.org>
- Pulitzer Prize—in the fields of biography, fiction, nonfiction, and poetry. Send four copies of the book, your photo, a short biography, and a $20 entry fee to the Pulitzer Committee, Graduate School of Journalism, 709 Journalism Building, Columbia University, 116th Street and Broadway, New York, New York 10027; (212) 854-3841 Home Page: <http://www.pulitzer.org>
- The Pushcart Prize—recognizes short stories. Contact them at P. O. Box 380, Wainscott, New York 11975; (516) 324-9300
- Spur Awards—formerly the Golden Spur Awards for ride 'em cowboy fiction and documentary novels. Contact Miles H. Swarthout, 29257 ½ Heathercliff Road, Malibu, CA 90265
- Violet Crown Book Awards—sponsored by the Austin Writers' League to honor three published books written by their members. Contact them at 1501 West Fifth Street, Suite E-2, Austin, TX 78703
- Western States Book Awards—recognizing poetry, fiction and nonfiction. Contact Western States Arts Federation, 1543 Champa Street, Suite 220, Denver,

CO 80202; (303) 629-1166, FAX: (303) 629-9717

- Writer's Digest Magazine—sponsors several awards throughout the year, including the Best Self-Published Award. 1507 Dana Avenue, Cincinnati, OH 45207; (513) 531-2690, ext. 580, FAX: (513) 531-1843

As you join organizations within your genre, you'll be introduced to specialty awards. The mystery genre, for example, offers top recognition including the Edgar, Agatha, Hammett, Shamus, Nero Wolfe, the Barry, and the Anthony. St. Martin's Press has the Best Mystery Award with cash and a publishing and promotional contract.

When you win—and you will, create embossed stickers promoting this award if the publisher doesn't.

In this extremely competitive publishing industry, your work will need to stand out in the crowd. Marketing is developing and retaining long term relationships. It's that "edge" you must nurture to succeed.

Find seminars on marketing. There are two outstanding groups in this area:

- The *Chicken Soup* team does an outstanding workshop that includes public speaking, *How to Build Your Speaking and Writing Empire—A Blueprint for Success*; a recommended must for ALL writers. Mark Victor Hansen Seminars, P. O. Box 7665, Newport Beach, CA 92658; (800) 433-2314, FAX: (949) 722-6912. Home Page: <www.*ChickenSoup*.com>
- Fred Pryor Seminars is another fine organization that offers a variety of presentations. P. O. Box 2951, Shawnee Mission, KS. 66201-1349 Workshop registration (800) 258-7246 or (800) 255-6139. Pryor

has a large selection of books, both audio and video, to help people improve skills.

Your work will have a greater survival rate if it's a series. Based on the theme of your work, align yourself with major organizations or businesses. Look at the cottage industry that the Canfield-Hansen group spawned with *Chicken Soup*. For example, they have a contract with IAMS, a major pet food manufacturer, to package their *Chicken Soup for the Pet Lover's Soul* with pet food. With a vitamin and herb organization they offer a copy of *Chicken Soup for the Enriching Soul* as a value-added product. Think beyond the box. Create a box like no other.

Set a Realistic Promotional Budget

So your publisher has promised an all-out promotional campaign that will make your book a blockbuster. Some houses will follow through; others will fall far short of your expectations.

The reality is that most publishers will spend more money on the printing of the book than they will on promotion. A national publisher will spend about $1,200 on a mid-list author, one who is not well-known in literary circles, or whose book is not destined to be a best-seller.

A regional or small press publisher may merely send out a few review copies and print a notice of your book in a catalog or two. Those are the cold hard facts.

Since you're dedicated to selling the first book and producing more, the budget you develop will drive the plan to succeed. As in every business, it takes money to make money.

Develop a separate budget of your own out-of-pocket

dollars that will allow you to:

- Travel
- Produce advertising materials
- Generate speaking engagements
- Schedule and attend signings

Include the set-up costs for your office and all equipment. Don't overlook maintenance, obsolescence, and replacement. Spend advertising dollars to create impressive press kits with professional photographs, handouts, and brochures. Those budget dollars may also include the hiring of a professional publicist.

If your novel sells nationwide, budget for:
- Travel expenses, including air
- Rental car, tolls and parking
- Telephone calls
- Meals

A significant amount of the budget is allocated to advertising materials and promotion. Budget on a yearly basis, broken into months, and even days.

When speaking to groups, if no honorarium is offered, ask them to reimburse all or part of your travel expenses. Make speaking fees flexible to fit the size of the group.

HINT: Use a credit card that generates Frequent Flyer miles. Save those miles for the longest trip to the biggest conference and go in style.

In 1970, at the Third Annual Clarion Science Fiction Workshop in Clarion, Pennsylvania, Harlan Ellison, a noted short story author, told a spell-bound audience, "Don't ever, ever give your work away. If you do, you'll be typecast as an amateur and nobody will ever want to pay you."

Almost thirty years later, he told eager writers at the Palm Springs Writer's Conference, "Don't give it away. You're a business. Charge for it. When you're not speaking, you're not writing. And when you're not writing, you aren't earning money."

As I shook my head and smiled, he looked me square in the eyes and said, "Spizer. Are you giving it away again?"

So I "charged" forth. Shortly after the conference I was invited to speak at a private women's club. I quoted them a $200 honorarium. The organizer said they didn't have that much money in their budget. She expected 100 to attend, so I suggested she add two dollars to the cost of the evening that included dinner. *Be creative. Make it a win-win.*

When speaking in small towns, ask the organizer for transportation to and from the airport to save on rental car costs. In one California community, the hostess was the Chief of Police and I rode in a police unit.

Often the hostess will invite friends in for potluck dinners to "Meet the Author." Books sell over dessert and coffee.

99

Budgeting begins while negotiating your publishing contract. Ask for the author's free copies, plus the freedom to purchase copies at a "discounted" price for marketing and sales use. Then ask for more free ones and a greater discount. No matter what the "contract" calls for, remember you can negotiate anything.

When asking for more, be ready to give solid evidence that it's in the best interest of the book and the publisher.

Those copies don't count toward your royalties. However, if that's a concern, find a local store. Ask them to order your books and sell them to you at their cost. This way they sell books and you receive royalties. You'll buy inexpensive copies that you, in turn, sell at full price. Another win-win.

The average cost you'll pay for these promotional books is generally the same price as bookstores pay: forty percent of the listed price. How many copies you ultimately use for promotion and how many you sell is up to you.

There are many items to consider in your marketing and promotional budget. Consider these basics when calculating start-up costs:

- Promotional materials
- Printing
- Postage and office supplies
- Travel
- Office maintenance
- State-of-the-art equipment
- Telephone, FAX and the Internet

Depending on your lifestyle, you may have to factor in other expenses. Do you need to provide for child care or for boarding Fido or Miss Kitty? Take into consideration all the provisions you must make before you embark on the promotional tour.

Let's talk about the dreaded two words we hate to hear: income taxes. Sometimes it isn't what you make, but what the IRS lets you keep, that's important. Whether you freelance, write novels, and/or teach, good record keeping is the edge to

17

increasing your share of the bucks.

Establish an author banking account. This simplifies checks written, and if you use a software accounting program, makes the year-end calculating as simple as a click on the screen.

If checks are written manually, it's best to purchase bookkeeping ledgers. One for income and one for expenses. Income includes book sales, royalty checks and honorarium, plus any additional "value-added" product you market.

Deductible expenses may include:
- Accounting fees
- Automobile expenses
- Conference, workshop and seminars
- Critique or reading fees, dues to professional organizations
- Equipment purchase, depreciation and maintenance
- Insurance
- Legal Fees
- Office expenses and supplies
- Postage, manuscript boxes and large sized envelopes
- Printing and copy costs
- Secretarial services, including typing and copying
- Taxes
- Travel and entertainment
- Utilities

Remember to keep an accurate record of all these expenses, especially travel. Most office supply stores carry mileage and expenditure logs to accurately record these costs. Some items will be fully tax deductible. A CPA or tax consultant is the best person to advise you. A professional can also suggest ways of record keeping that will save hours and dollars at tax time.

How much money will you need to spend? Peter Lance, author of *First Degree Burn*, spent $4,032 of his own money to produce 1,200 promotional copies of the $5.99 mystery paperback. Through September 1997, when a *Wall Street Journal* article was written about his marketing plan, he had spent $34,762 of his own money to spotlight his work among the 55,000 titles published that year.

It's worth repeating: it takes money to make money. Although most of us don't have that kind of money to spend on promotion, a good rule of thumb is to plan on spending almost all of your royalty checks and advance. Most of these will be up-front expenses, but are often tax deductible against your income.

Establishing a Promotional Time-line

The publication schedule drives the book's promotion. Most publishers produce a spring and fall catalog. Remember, your book will be competing with thousands of others being published during the same period of time. Unless you are fortunate enough to be a celebrity and have lots of money for marketing and promotion, you must work smarter than the others to make your book stand out.

Let's assume you're not a major author, yet. Ask your house to publish off season, when you're not competing with blockbuster authors. You'll need the edge.

The time frame between the contract and printing of the book is prime time to position your book for the market.

A bit of ingenuity on your part will help position the book for the highest market exposure.

19

Timing may not be everything, but it's important. Try to schedule the publication date to coincide with a significant time in history relating to the work. For instance, if the book is a biography of a major literary figure, coordinate with her or his birthday. A dessert cookbook with lots of gooey delights? Catch the Thanksgiving and Christmas seasons. A children's book featuring rabbits? Perfect for book tables before Easter.

If the setting of your latest crime thriller is a New England fall, advertising and sales plans should be in place by September when the leaves are beginning to turn. Murder at a seaside resort? Have the novel available by late May so it's the first book vacationers tuck into their travel bags.

If your life has been devastated by sorrow, do what the newspapers do for sensationalism, "catch the exploitation buzz." After the Columbine High School tragedy in April 1999, the mother of victim Cassie Bernall popped a hardback out in ninety days.

According to the July 1999 *Wall Street Journal's* article on Bernall's book, super agent Jonathon Lazear said, "I'm marketing virtually everything you can exploit, and I mean that in a positive way." Misty Bernall's publicists and agents:

- Booked her on the network's talk show circuit
- Placed the book in mass market stores like Wal-Mart, K-Mart, and Costco
- Shopped the story around Hollywood
- Taped an inspirational video
- Excerpted the book for major magazines
- Sold book-club rights
- Created a web site where teens could share feelings
- Sold European rights

- Considered setting up a charitable foundation with proceeds from the book

The Direct Marketing Association reports that the best months for promotions are in January, February, October, August, November, and September—in that order. But that doesn't mean that a book on bunny rabbits shouldn't be hopping into stores in time for Easter. Or a book on patriotism shouldn't be in stores in time for July 4th.

Bookstores set their Christmas promotions early and do no direct mailings after November 13th. With the holidays and the increased mail-flow, don't get lost in the seasonal rush. The next best date for promotional mailings is January 2nd.

Maybe Richard Paul Evans' *Christmas Box* will sell all year long, but that's an exception to the rules.

Getting Those All-Important Reviews

The minute your publisher sends you galley proofs to correct, plan book reviews. These professional critiques are critical to the book's success. The publisher should mail at least five hundred review copies at least ninety days before the official "pub date." Ask the editor/publisher for a copy of his list and verification of the date the books were mailed.

Use your reviewer list and send out one hundred more. Copies may be bound, or for advance review copies (ARC), send galleys. Verify, however, that the reviewers will read from galleys. To avoid duplication, double check your roster against that of the publishing house. Rubber stamp them as review copies so they won't be sold as new books.

Below is a list of the major players in the book review media. As with any address and telephone listing in a published book, always call first to verify accuracy of the information. The publishing industry is constantly on the move. With one telephone call, ask for a copy of their submission guidelines, the name of the review editor for your genre, and check their address.

Send a galley to that person's attention. On the envelope, write "REQUESTED MATERIAL." These two all-important words may keep you from being unceremoniously dumped on the slush pile.

Don't waste time or expense sending it Return Receipt Requested, Certified Mail, or Overnight. The package is opened in a mail room by someone who doesn't have time to read, placed in a bin for that specific editor, and later transported to the bottom of his or her slush pile.

A cover letter should accompany the galley. It must be compelling and dramatic enough to cause the editor/reviewer to read it. Pattern the letter after your query letter—one page with lots of punch. Don't forget to mention the "pub date."

The editor/reviewer needs to know, without looking on the copyright page, how long he/she has to read and review the book before publication, to give you the best possible market exposure.

Their magazines and newspapers have deadlines too. If it's received too late, you've lost that edge.

Book Sense is a newly created venture of the American Booksellers Association. Its unique program offers online and in-store marketing and promotion for participating independent book stores. It's the American Booksellers Association's answer to Amazon.com and other online book retailers.

• With information gathered from an association of over

1,000 stores, compiles a top ten list of recommended reads
- Book stores can customized web sites, and link with authors
- Focuses on small press releases
- Publishes *Bookselling This Week*, a newsletter about the independent marketplace
- Tour the BookSense.com prototype at <www.bookweb.org>
- Offers co-op advertising between the publishing house and the book stores
- Contact Book Sense at ABA, 828 S. Broadway, Tarrytown, New York 10591, (800) 637-0037, ext 1269 E-mail: <carl@booksense.com>

General Book Reviewers

- *Association of College and Research Libraries* is located at 50 East Huron Street, Chicago, Ill 60611; (312) 280-2517 or (800) 545-2433, FAX: (312) 280-2520. E-mail: <acrl@ala.org> or <http://www.ala.org/acrl/html>
- *Booklist*—a bi-weekly publication of the American Library Association. They review 10,000 books a year. They're located at American Library Association, 50 E. Huron Street, Chicago, IL 60611; (800) 545-2433, FAX: (312) 944-8741. Home Page: <http://www.ala.org>
- *Choice*—is published eleven times a year by the Association of College and Research Libraries. This journal reviews more than 7,500 books designed as college library books for undergraduate students.

23

Contact them at 100 Riverview Center, Middletown, CT 06457. (203) 347-6933

- *Deadly Pleasures Magazine*—for those in the mystery genre, publishes four times a year. Contact George Easter at P. O. Box 969, Bountiful, UT 84011. (801) 2 9 9 - 9 4 3 3 . O r e - m a i l h i m a t <george@deadlypleasures.com>

- *Horn Book Magazine*--is published bi-monthly for all categories of children's literature. This is the most prestigious reviewer of children's books in the United States. Librarians often make their purchases direct from Horn's reviews. It's a privilege to have your book reviewed favorably in this magazine. They review over 500 books a year. Contact them at 11 Beacon Street, Boston, MA 02108; (617) 227-1555 or (800) 325-1170. FAX: (617) 523-0299. E-mail: <info@hbook.com> or <www.hbook.com>

- *Kirkus Reviews*—is published bi-weekly and reviews 100 books per issue. They don't review poetry, mass-market paperbacks, or children's picture books. Contact them at 200 Park Avenue South, #1118, New York, New York 10003-1543; (212) 979-1352. E-mail: <kirkusrevs@aol.com>

- *Library Journal*—is published monthly for the nation's public library system. They review over 6,000 books a year, with the exception of textbooks, children's books and technical books. Send your book to them at 245 West 17th Street, New York, New York, 10011. Telephone: (212) 463-6819, FAX: (212) 463-6734 or (212) 463-6631. E-<mail:awright@ljcahners.com> or <http://www.ljdigital.com>

- *Publishers Weekly*—the writer's trade magazine. They review over 5,000 books per year. This publication is the pulse of the publishing industry. Mark your submission attention *PW FORECASTS* and send to 245 West 17th Street, New York, New York 10011. (212) 463-6758, FAX: (212) 463-6631
- *School Library Journal*—publishes ten times a year corresponding with the school calendar, and reviews 3,000 books. Contact Cahners Magazine, 245 West 17th Street, New York, New York 10011. (212) 463-6759, FAX: (212) 463-6689. E-mail: <slj@cahners.com> or <http://www.slj.com>

State-Wide or Regional Book Reviewers

Each state or region has one or two book-review services that focus on books dealing with their specific region. Be sure to contact them for guidelines on submitting galleys or the published book.

Several services include:
- Review of Texas Books, P. O. Box 10021, Beaumont, Texas 77710. (409) 880-8118
- Books of the Southwest, 201 W. Polk Street, Sabinal, Texas 78881; (830) 988-2566, FAX: (830) 278-3339. E-mail: <frichter@sul-ross-l.sulross.edu>
- Small Press Review, Box 100, Paradise, CA 95967; (530) 877-6110 or (800) 477-6110. FAX: (530) 877-0222. E-mail: <dustbooks@telis.org>

Newspaper and Magazine Reviewers

Begin by contacting your local newspaper and throwaway papers. If your book garners a major newspaper review, that not only spells sales, it's one way to get your book title before many of the major bookstore chains.

Here are a few book review sources:

- *Chicago Tribune Books*—a Sunday section for general interest reviews. Contact them at 435 N. Michigan Avenue, Room 400, Chicago, IL 66011-4022. (312) 222-3232, FAX: (312) 222-4760
- *Esquire Magazine*—has over 700,000 readers. Send galleys to Adrienne Miller at Hearst Group, 250 West 55th Street, New York, New York 10019. (212) 649-4020
- *GQ Magazine*—has over 700,000 readers. Send galleys to Lee Smith or Suzannah Meadows at 4 Times Square, New York, New York 10036. (212) 880-8800
- *Los Angeles Times Book Review*—a Sunday supplement that reviews over 2,500 books a year. Times Mirror Square, Los Angeles, CA 90053.(213) 237-5000 or (800) 528-4637, FAX: (213) 237-4712 (edit), (213) 237-5493, (communs). Home Page: <http://www.latimes.com>
- *Newsweek*—has a 3.2 million reader circulation. Send galleys well in advance to Jeff Giles, Ray Sawhill, or David Alpern at 251 West 57th Street, New York, New York 10019. (212) 445-4000. Web site: <www.newsweek.com>
- *New York Newsday*—a daily reviewer of general interest novels. Their address is Two Park Avenue, New York, New York 10016. (212) 251-6623, FAX: (212) 696-0590. Home Page: <http://www.newsday.com>
- *New York Review of Books*—published biweekly and

reviews 1,500 novels. Contact them at NYREV, Inc. 1755 Broadway, 5th Floor, New York, New York 10019; (212) 757-8070, FAX: (212) 333-5374

- *New York Times Book Review*—the supplement to the Sunday edition of the *New York Sunday Times*, reviews over 4,000 books each year. For guidelines, write them at 229 West 43rd Street, New York, New York 10036. Telephone: (800) 631-2580, FAX: (212) 556-7088

- *Playboy*—reaches 3.2 million readers monthly. Send galleys to Barbara Nellis at 680 North Lake Shore Drive, Chicago, Il, 60611. (312) 751-8000

- *San Francisco Chronicle Book Review*—does 1,500 reviews per year in the Sunday *Chronicle*. Their address is 275 Fifth Street, San Francisco, CA 94103. (415) 777-7043, FAX: (415) 957-8737

- *San Francisco Review of Books*—a bimonthly magazine with special interest on novels published on the west coast. Contact them at P. O. Box 33-0090, San Francisco, CA 94133. (415) 543-7372

- *Time Magazine*—a 4 million readership each week makes this a worthwhile effort to get reviewed. Contact: Marianne Sussman at Time & Life Building, Rockefeller Center, New York, New York 10020. (212) 522-1212. Web site: <www.time.com>

- *USA Today*—published five times a week. Contact them at 1000 Wilson Boulevard, Arlington, VA 22209. (703) 276-3400.

- *USA Weekend*—reaches 43 million readers a week as a newspaper insert throughout the United States. Send galleys to Constance Kurz at 1000 Wilson Blvd, Arlington, VA 22229. (703) 276-6445

- *U.S. News and World Report*—a 2.1 million circulation will help your sales if you can break into this magazine. Contact them at 1050 Thomas Jefferson Street, Washington, D.C. 20007. (202) 955-2000. Web site: <www.usnews.com> Send books, galleys and catalogs to Wray Herbert at <wherbert@usnews.com> and Holly Morris at <hmorris@usnews.com>
- *Voice Literary Supplement*—a monthly supplement of the *Village Voice* newspaper. Contact them at 36 Cooper Square, New York, New York 10003. (212) 475-3333, FAX: (212) 475-8944
- *Washington Post Book World*—is the supplement to the *Sunday Post* and reviews 2,500 books per year. Their address is 1150 15th Street, NW, Washington, D.C. 20071. (202) 334-6000

In addition to these publications, most states have an association of newspapers or media sources. You can obtain names and addresses of newspapers in your state or region that review books from the *LMP* or *Ulrich's International Periodical Directory*. Don't overlook specialty sources, like airline magazines that often have book reviews. And not all publications review books, so don't do a statewide mailing. Be selective in those you choose.

Small Press Reviewers
As the publishing industry shrinks, small presses are gaining a larger and more respectful share of the market. Each year 5,000 new small publishing houses are established. If your book is being published by a small press or if you are self-publishing

under your own imprint, check out these sources for reviews:

- *Bloomsbury Review*—a bimonthly publication featuring reviews of small press titles. Contact them through Owaissa Communications, Inc. 1762 Emerson Street, Denver, CO 80218. (303) 863-0406 or (800) 783-3338, FAX: (303) 863-0408. E-Mail: <bloomsb@aol.com>
- *Independent Publisher Magazine*—a bimonthly magazine reviews 100 books an issue. They can be reached at 121 East Front Street, Suite 301, Traverse City, Mich 49684. (800) 706-4636
- *Small Press*—a quarterly magazine reviews 150 to 200 titles an issue. Contact them at Moyer Bell, Kymbolde Way, Wakefield, RI 02879.(888) 789-1945, FAX: (401) 789-3793. E-mail: <sales@moyerbell.com< or <http://www.moyerbell.com>
- *Small Press Book Review*—a bimonthly newsletter that reviews 100 titles per issue. Contact them at P.O. Box 176, Southport, CT 06490. Telephone and FAX (203) 332-7629. E-mail: <henryberry@aol.com>
- *Small Press Review*—is the original periodical that reviews primarily literary fiction and poetry in its monthly issues. Contact them at Dustbooks, P. O. Box 100, Paradise, CA 95969. (530) 877-6110 or (800) 477-6110. FAX: (530) 877-0222. E-mail: <dustbooks@telis.org>
-

Specialty Reviewers
There are many review services for special interests and genres. Here are a few:

- *Black Issues Book Review*—reviews 30 to 40 books bi-monthly. Send galleys to the Kristina Nwazota, Managing Editor, Empire State Building, 350 Fifth Avenue, Suite 7720, New York, New York 10018. (212) 947-8794. FAX: (212) 947-5674. E-mail: <kristina@cmabiccw.com>
- *Bookviews* – a syndicated column reaching newspapers across the country and the Internet. They prefer the actual book, not the galley, and require little lead time. Alan Caruba, editor of *Bookviews,* is a charter member of the National Book Critics Circle, contact him at Caruba Organization, 9 Brookside Road, Box 40, Maplewood, New Jersey 07040; (973) 972-5600; <acaruba@aol.com>
- *Catholic News Service*—is a wire service covering 180 Catholic newspapers in the United States and 40 predominately English-speaking countries. Review coordinator Richard Philbrick reviews one book a week in a column entitled *Books En Route*. The service also produces several specials: before Christmas and at the close of the school year. There's another monthly column *The Reading Room* written by Joseph R. Thomas. Contact them at 3211 4th Street, NE, Washington, D.C. 20017; (202) 541-3271. Joseph R. Thomas at 18 Cypress Avenue, Vernon, New Jersey, 07044
- *Feminist Bookstore News*—a bimonthly newsletter that circulates to over 400 feminist bookstores throughout the world. You can reach them at P. O. Box 882554, San Francisco, CA 94188. (415) 626-1556, FAX: (415) 626-8970. E-mail: <fbn@fembknews.com>

- *New Age Retailer*—a trade journal for new-age booksellers with a circulation of over 5,500. Contact them through Continuity Publishing at 1300 North State Street, Suite 105, Bellingham, WA 98225; (800) 463-9243, FAX: (360) 676-0932. E-mail: <newagere@pacificrim.net>
- *New York City (NYC) Magazine*—a quarterly metro magazine for New Yorkers, conducts book reviews, but a NYC connection is not necessary. Contact publisher George Levy at 430 Park Avenue, 2nd Floor, New York, New York 10022. (212) 750-3333
- *Notorious*—has a circulation of 100,000 reviews 4 or 5 books per bi-monthly issue. They also interview authors. Send galleys to Eva Nagorski, Senior Editor, 37 East 28th Street, Suite 906, New York, New York 10016. (212) 685-7837. FAX: (212) 685-7831
- *Romantic Times*—a monthly book review magazine targeting the romance market. If your book is romance, this is the magazine for you. Contact them at 55 Bergen Street, Brooklyn Heights, New York, New York 11201. (718) 237-1097, FAX: (718) 624-4231
- *Sci/Tech Book News*—reviews highly technical, scientific, and medical books. They are published ten times a year. Contact them at 5739 NE Summer Street, Portland, OR 97218; (503) 281-9230, FAX: (503) 287-4485. E-mail: <booknews@booknews.com>
- *Sleuthhound Magazine*—reviews mysteries. Published quarterly, contact them at 2517 South Central, P. O. Box 890294, Oklahoma City, OK 73189-0294, (405) 239-2531. FAX: (405) 236-0502. E-mail: <wwillow@telepath.com>

- *Working at Home*– a quarterly with over 300,000 circulation. Reviews four books each issue. Send galleys to Jodie Green or David Carnoy at 733 Third Avenue, New York, New York 10017. (212) 883-7100. FAX: (212) 949-7002

For additional book review sources, check *Literary Market Place* or *Ulrich's International Periodical Directory*. Look for those sources that review in your genre and have a good circulation. Don't face embarrassment. Locate and read several issues of those magazines or newsletters to make sure you have a match. This will increase your odds of being reviewed.

There's a wonderful market for increasing sales in Book Clubs. Check out the *Literary Market Place* to identify clubs like Science Fiction, Doubleday, Book Club of the Month, Detective Book Club, Writer's Digest Book Club and hundreds more.

F&W Publishing operates five clubs: Decorative Arts, Graphic Designers, North Light (for fine arts and painting), Woodworkers, and Writer's Digest Book Clubs. Send your book to Julia Groh at 1507 Dana Avenue, Cincinnati, OH 45207. (513) 531-2222, or (513) 531-2690, ext 249. FAX: (513) 531-7107. E-mail <julia@fwpubs.com>

Now is a good time to meet the community service representative with the larger chains. Either mail your galley and some press information, a press kit, or your business card, and a flyer on the book, to their personal attention, or take a set by the store. Introduce yourself and ask if they'd like a preview of a book that will sell like hot-cakes for them.

Be sure to alert them to the book's publication date and tell them you are available for signings. This initial visit is only the first, so make it a memorable one. Be cordial and enthusiastic about your book. Answer all questions with confidence. Be sure to collect the owner or representative's card and a telephone number where they can be reached for a follow-up call.

Remember, these professionals are your links to the book-buying public, so make a good impression.

All this talk about calling strangers and scheduling meetings making you a bit nervous? You never thought of yourself as a salesperson, did you? Don't worry. Turn the page for your next journey.

2

Heavens . . .
How Can I Ever Give a Speech?

How many times do authors express their anxiety about public speaking? How many times do we answer, "Oh, yes, you can do this." And you must if you're ever going to sell a book.

You can't hide behind the computer any longer. The book will not sell itself. The world wants to see you and touch you and talk with you. You've pulled yourself away from the non-published writers. They yearn to learn how you did it. They want to do it too. You're now an expert and people want to hear your story. How'd you do it?

Developing your public persona is another key to your success as an author. No one can promote this work better than you.

Speaking before a group may sound daunting, even scary. But it's easy to master the art. The secret is practice, practice, practice. And then practice some more.

Before you embark on your first speaking tour, try inviting a group of close friends in to hear your presentation.

Work on creating your individual "sound bytes."

What works and what doesn't? Ask for critiques that will help you present yourself before strangers. Write down the things you want and need to work on.

Try the power of meditation, daily affirmations, and/or prayer. They are important to the "chi" balance of mind and body. They help with relaxation and opens your energy with both force and humor.

If you still feel uneasy, help is at hand in your community. There are professional organizations, such as The Toastmasters, who can help even the most faint-hearted speak well in public. Most colleges and universities, both state and community, offer basic courses on public speaking. Many allow you to audit these classes.

Join your local little theater, even if you have to sew costumes or usher. Listen and learn. These provide excellent forums to help you learn to "think on your feet."

Speak before members of a senior activity center. They're a great audience and so appreciative.

Offer a free speech to a youth club, a group of volunteers, or to church groups. Ask for feedback. Ask what they liked and how they thought you could improve. You might even sell a few books.

The following steps will guide you toward the podium with confidence, clarity, and calm. Don't strive to be just a good speaker, become a great one:

Step One: Be Prepared
Confirm your appearance, the time, and the location in advance. Embarrassments like showing up on the wrong date, time, or place has happened to authors in the past and will again. One

book store moved before the signing and didn't notify the author. Bring a written introduction even though your press kit was mailed long ago. Better to have two copies of your introduction, than none, if the host misplaces your papers.

Discuss your presentation with the organizer. Make sure you have enough hand-outs for all the anticipated guests and, of course, plenty of books.

Know your audience and what they expect from your presentation. What are the demographics of the audience? Are you sharing creative writing tools, talking about your career, or inspiring others?

If this is a question-and-answer program give your presenter a pre-selected list of questions that you believe the audience would like answered. If you've spoken more than once, you're already starting to hear the questions repeated. Your answers are getting stronger.

Need props? Always ask about the size of the room and what equipment is available: Microphone, overhead projector, easel, screen. Don't wait until the last minute to need important pieces of equipment. And, when you arrive, test it. Outlets short out. Batteries die. Life happens. Be prepared. Adjust and overcome.

On presentation day give yourself ample time to locate the site and park. Plan on arriving at least thirty to forty-five minutes early for set-up time.

There is nothing that makes you feel more at ease than knowing your material. The elements to success as a public speaker whether you entertain, inform, or educate, are to practice, practice, practice. That's the whole secret. Speaking in a clear, articulate voice is your goal.

Write out your speech, or work from note cards.

Whatever makes you feel comfortable. Nothing takes the place of knowing your material thoroughly. However, don't try to memorize the presentation. That makes it sound wooden and "stilted."

You don't have to follow the written text exactly, but at least have an outline, notes, or speech cards to cue you. They help you stay on track. Remember your time constraints and don't abuse them. And always allow extra time in the event you're asked to remain longer.

Step Two: Speak with Enthusiasm and Warmth

No one knows your book better than you do. No one has fallen in love with those characters; no one knows their feelings and motivations like you.

Now, make your audience believe in your book enough to buy it. Practice before a mirror, not only for the clarity of delivery, but the timing as well. Watch those facial expressions. Rehearse over and over again, removing the "uh," and local phrases that detract, "like, you know." Try not to look terrified, even if you are. Be sure to smile at the audience. A bright, twinkling smile and a voice that conveys warmth will bring your audience to you and result in increased book sales.

If you're nervous, don't feel well, or have personal problems, like car trouble or a sick child—keep it to yourself. Above all, do not apologize. It won't bring the audience to your side and causes embarrassment for you, the audience, and the organizer.

Tape yourself on a cassette recorder and play those tapes back. Work for improvement in your speaking technique and don't stop working. Time spent working from the tapes in your hotel room the night before you speak, is time well spent.

Then use a videocassette to study your speaking posture and your technique. If money is no object, hire a media trainer to polish your image and develop those "sound bytes."

Step Three: The Early Bird Gets the Book Sales

Arrive early at your speaking site. In advance, ask for a long cloth-covered table set up near the entrance to display books. Check to make sure it's there.

On it, arrange your posters, handout materials, flyers, a few business cards, and your books. Stand one or two upright to catch the audience's attention at the door. Stack plenty of books on the table, or they'll think you have only a few to sell. Better to carry unsold books home, than to miss a sale.

You have a travel bag, right? These are items you'll find indispensable:

- One or two hand-held calculators
- A bag from your local bank to keep checks and money in
- A supply of one-dollar bills
- Five or six of your favorite pens for book signing
- A credit-card machine, if you have one. Set it up and prominently display it on the table. On it:
- Arrange legible small signs with the price of your book or books and how the buyers are to make out checks near the book stacks
- Have a pad of paper or small pieces of paper available. Have people print the name they want and hand it to you with the book open to the signature page, or stick the piece on the autograph page.
- Display the price(s) on the poster

Ask the event coordinator to have a person available at the table to help with the book signing and collect payments. He or she will open your book to the page to be signed and pass it to you. This expedites the line and gives you a more professional appearance.

Check out the equipment in advance. Microphones vary and so do the height of speakers. Be sure the microphone is positioned for you and look carefully at its location. If the person who introduces you changes the position of the microphone, move it to the correct spot before you begin speaking. Also, be sure the volume is adjusted to a position where you can be heard across the room. Be sure there are no squeals, hums, or other noises to distract the audience from the presentation.

HINT: I like to use a lavaliere microphone when possible. It allows me to roam, covering the stage, gesturing, and walking close to the audience. This makes each person feel part of my story.

Avoid alcohol the night before the event, get plenty of sleep, and practice deep breathing. Be sure to have an adequate breakfast with some protein. You don't want to pass out at the podium.

Eat sparingly of the luncheon or dinner menu and avoid eating anything too rich or spicy. If you're the least bit nervous, these foods tend to accelerate nerves. Ask the wait-person to leave your dessert for you, and eat it after the book signing.

Prepare your introduction in advance, and mail it to the

presenter. When you arrive at the site, go over it with them so there are no mistakes. Have an extra copy of your introduction with you, in case he or she left it at home by the microwave.

Make the introduction short and sweet. Now is the time for your "sound byte." Focus on the reason you're there. No one cares how many advanced degrees you have or if you are a great friend to pets. However, if you've recently won a major award for writing, be sure to mention it.

Leave the folder or envelope of note cards at the podium before you speak. Then it's ready to open when you arrive at the podium.

When the audience arrives, mingle with everyone you can. Greet these prospective buyers and introduce yourself. Make one or two comments about the books and encourage them to look before your presentation. People like to ask informal questions during this time. Be prepared to answer them.

Sometimes you can stand copies of the book or books on the tables near the centerpiece. Encourage the audience to look through the books while the wait-persons are serving.

This isn't possible with a large group, but it focuses a small group's attention on what you're there to talk about. Nine times out of ten, someone at the table will buy the book.

HINT: Depending on the size of the group, offer a first edition copy of the book as a door prize. That generates funds for the organization hosting the program and gets the novel in a new reader's hands.

If I'm invited to a private home, I wrap a book in black silk ribbon and take it as hostess gift.

Either way, post that book in the record log as a gift, not a sale. No sales tax to collect or pay.

99

Step Four: "Speak the Speech, I Pray You . . ."

Now is the time when all your practice pays off. The presenter has introduced you and the applause is loud and long. You walk to the podium with confidence. Smile at your audience.

Don't let your terror show, even if your knees are shaking. Stand tall at the dais, position your feet comfortably, legs slightly apart.

Do not grip the podium for dear life. It's not going anywhere. However, if the dias gives you stability, rest your hands lightly on it.

Don't rustle papers nor pick up any nervous habits like removing and replacing your glasses, or tapping a pen. Noises carry.

Take a deep breath and begin. Thank the presenter for his or her kind words. Briefly acknowledge the audience for inviting you with a personalized "thank you." "It's great to be here in Miami again and speak to you about my favorite topic." (Be sure you are in Miami and not Midland.) "It's wonderful to be here to speak to Sisters-in-Crime, a great organization and tremendous supporter of my book."

Begin your speech with a riveting topic sentence designed to draw your audience into your book, why you wrote it, and the way you wrote it.

HINT: A "sound byte" from your former profession is an excellent way to introduce the speech. One of mine is, "I saw my first dead body when I was twenty-one years old." That always gets an audience's attention and makes them want to know more about me and my book.

If you're speaking to a group of writers or pre-published authors, a quote from Ray Bradbury helps break the ice and speaks to reality. "I wrote a million words before I wrote one good one."

If you flub a line, and we all do, do not apologize or get flustered. Keep going. You may have a chance later in your speech to slip in a correction. But make it short and don't draw attention to it. A good sense of humor will carry you through any difficulty in this area.

HINT: At a California book-club luncheon, a female presenter rose to introduce Los Angeles Chief of Police Darryl Gates, who was speaking on his new autobiography, *Chief*.

In her enthusiasm, she said, "It's my pleasure to introduce the biggest cock in the Los Angeles Police Department, Chief Darryl Gates."

The audience roared, but the presenter had no idea what she had said. Chief Gates walked up to the microphone, smiled, and graciously replied, "Yes, I am, thank you."

And the house roared again.

Recite facts and examples, anecdotes, and stories that relate to the book and your experiences.

Don't be afraid to use humor. Be sure, however, the humor is appropriate to the topic and the group. What's funny to the Rodeo Club might seem inappropriate to the Methodist women in your community. Pause after you've said something funny. Enjoy it with the audience. Don't rush your presentation.

Eye contact is most important. You may choose two or three people sitting in different areas of the room and direct your comments to them. Let your eyes sweep from one to the other. Cover the entire room. Or, if looking into the eyes of the audience terrifies you, look slightly over their heads. Don't, however, stare at the ceiling. Your script isn't rolling on cue cards up there.

Focus on the audience. As you become a more practiced speaker, you will learn how to draw the audience to you. Personal touches, even a joke on yourself, make the audience anxious to read your book.

Study other speakers and adapt techniques from them that suit your speaking style. Notice timing, rhythm, and pauses. Appreciate eye contact and facial expressions.

Use appropriate gestures that keep the audience focused on you. Often moving a hand from your body toward the audience shows compassion. Gesturing with an outstretched hand brought into the body brings the audience to you. Don't overdo gestures; waving your arms like a windmill detracts from good speaking techniques.

Be animated, passionate and enthusiastic about your speech. Love your audience. As you become a practiced speaker, learn to like these people. After all, they must be nice folks--they came to hear what you have to say. Learn to appreciate each group and what they have to offer.

If this is a large group ask a monitor to stand or give you a hand motion when you have five minutes left. You have practiced the timing beforehand, of course, but this will give you more security. The more often you present this program, the more proficient you will become.

End your speech on an upbeat note. This doesn't mean saying, "Hey, murder's great. Read all about it," but an ending that focuses on the great characters in your novel, the practical aspects of your "how-to" book, what you can learn from the events in your book on local history.

If your program lends itself to questions and answers later, apportion that time, giving forthright and honest answers. People like a back-and-forth discussion with an author. But, don't let one person monopolize your time. Make sure you can conclude your presentation, answer everyone's questions, and allow yourself plenty of time to sign books.

Step Five: Savor the Applause; Sell Those Books

The best speakers will sell themselves, not the book. The audience came to hear you. Through your presentation they'll learn more about you and like you. The book will sell itself.

If a meeting is to follow your presentation, quietly slip from the head table and sit or stand at the book-signing table, right behind your books, a smile on your face.

If a crowd has gathered at the book-signing area, a gentle nudge at the conclusion of your presentation may stimulate book sales. "Come on over to the signing table so we can talk more."

Make book-signing a personal statement. As you hand the book to the buyer, thank her or him and tell each you hope they enjoy it. "I hope you enjoy reading my book as much as I enjoyed writing it," is one way of saying thanks. A gracious "thank you" always garners repeat sales and fond memories of you as a speaker.

HINT: I pre-autograph my books--in black ink--at home, long before the event, for buyers who don't want a book personalized or who want to grab a book and run. This guarantees that you never miss a sale. For those wanting the book dedicated, all you add is the date and the dedication. This allows time to talk with each customer and make that a personal moment between you and your new fan. You never know who might prove to be the contact person for your next speaking engagement.

Well, you did it. You made it through a speech and a book signing. Your face hurts from smiling, your feet ache, and your throat is dry and raspy. But you made it. And what a success. No one stood up and "booed." No one rushed from the room to avoid your works; and you've autographed a zillion books.

And that's the first zillion. Book signings often result in repeat sales and new contacts. After all, the word is out--you're a terrific speaker.

Now it's time to repair the damage. Hauling books around takes a lot out of you. Your throat is a precious instrument that helps you sell books, and you must rest and rejuvenate it. Not to mention those aching feet.

If you're on an extended book tour, it's even more important that you preserve your voice. When you travel, always ask your hotel or motel for a quiet, smoke-free room. Now is your time to unwind.

Take off your clothes and those wretched shoes. Retire to your yoga mat or use the pool and exercise equipment.

Treat yourself to room service. You deserve it. Order some hot tea with honey or a light supper. Use your throat spray or simply gargle with warm salt water. Relax, savor your moment--and get ready for the next speaking engagement.

HINT: When you're on the road, even for a short overnight stay, take a goodie bag. Keep plastic bags packed with herb tea, small jars of honey, small plastic salt shakers, throat lozenges, and a bottle of throat spray.

Tuck in quick-energy snacks, such as raisins or dried cranberries. Ginseng and St. John's Wort always travel with me, as does Valerin if I'm traveling by plane. Speaking takes it out of you. Rejuvenation is as close as your pharmacy or health-food store.

With a bubble bath, a good foot rub with peppermint foot cream, and a restful night's sleep, I'm good as new the next day--and raring to speak and sell those books.

I always carry night eye shades and ear plugs. And I never leave home without my cervical pillow. We don't need a sleepless night and a headache to mar the next day's presentation.

In addition to my daily vitamins and minerals, I pack emergency supplies of aspirin, nose drops, allergy pills, bandaids, eye drops, and cold medication. At the slightest hint of a throat infection brought on by the dust mites in air conditioning filters on airplanes and in airless hotel rooms, I take medication that the doctor prescribes.

And I always carry small bottles of water. I drink lots of water. It reduces the swelling in your limbs and helps the voice. There's nothing so dehydrating as the recycled air in planes, hotels, and conference rooms.

99

For the next several years—and the next several books—you're going to be speaking, speaking, speaking. To all kinds of groups in all sorts of places. Sometimes the experience won't be enjoyable—in fact, you may prepare for hours, speak to a full house, and not sell a single book. You'll face hecklers. Your hair spray will fail and so will your deodorant. You'll find runs in your hose, or worse—you packed one black shoe and one blue shoe. Life happens.

From now until the day you stop writing, however, it will be part of your life. Learn to enjoy it. Continue to improve your speaking techniques.

Learn which of your anecdotes or stories your audiences appreciate the most. Work to create suspense and interest about your book and your writing.

Soon you're a world-class speaker—selling those books.

Step 6: What makes a speech successful?
A successful speech has several parts:
- It begins as a concept, an idea, a central thesis. Who is your audience? Why are you there? What is your dowry to the program?
- Add structure, weaving and building on the core. Like telling a story that's revealed a page at a time.

- Create a "sound byte" that will be remembered long after you've left the podium. Who can forget, "Give me liberty, or give me death." Or "Ask not what your country can do for you..." Or "I have a dream." At Gettysburg, November 19, 1863, Abraham Lincoln spoke for less than three minutes; Edward Everett's speech lasted two hours. Which speech do you remember?
- Weave the presentation until the cloth is complete.
- End with a bang and make them beg for more.
- Tell them you're going to tell them something. Tell them. Then tell them you told them.

No matter how experienced you are at public speaking, always outline the presentation. Then tighten, trim words, rehearse, and tighten it again. Listen to yourself and you'll hear what works and what doesn't. Practice for the family, the mirror, or close friends. Listen for constructive criticism. You're doing this for several reasons:

- To hear the weak spots
- To memorize bits and pieces
- To test the time-line. There's nothing so boring as a thirty minute speaker dragging on for almost an hour.

Transitions and humor are excellent changes to test audience attention. Don't be cute, unless you can carry it off. There's only one Bill Cosby.

Symbols, metaphors, and quotations bring the audience on the ride you're taking. The key is customizing those to your speech. If they're Democrats, don't quote a Republican. Don't quote William Buckley, when it should be Gore Vidal. Know your audience.

Several recommended speech sources are:

- *Bartlett's Famous Quotations* by John Bartlett
- *Secrets of Successful Speakers* by Lilly Walters
- *The Greatest Speakers I Ever Heard* by Dottie Walters

Don't miss *How to Build Your Speaking and Writing Empire* presented by Mark Hanson and Jack Canfield, our *Chicken Soup* friends. It's the most powerful weekend you'll ever invest in. Contact Mark Victor Hansen Seminars, P. O. Box 7665, Newport Beach, CA 92658; (800) 433-2314, FAX (949) 722-6912. Home Page: <www.*ChickenSoup*.com>

If your budget includes media training dollars, remember the more exposure you have, the more books fly off the shelves. Highly trained image professionals cost big bucks, so unless you want to tape an infomercial, you're better off having family members tape you or stand in front of a mirror and practice.

You can buy an excellent video entitled *You're on the Air* from Marketing Directions, Inc., P. O. Box 715, Avon, CT 06001-0715. FAX (860) 676-0759 if you're serious about media training, kits, and much more.

Padgett Thompson, a Division of American Management Association at P O Box 8297, Overland Park, KS 66208, offers an inexpensive one-day seminar, *How to Plan, Write and Edit Video Scripts*. Telephone 1-800-255-4141.

Speak and get paid for it. Dottie Walters is Editor-in-Chief of one of the world-renowned speaker bureaus, Walters Speakers Bureau. She knows how to help you find those paying customers. Send a one page, how-to article to *Sharing Ideas*, her magazine for entrepreneurial speakers. You are automatically represented by her firm when they print your article. Contact Lois Shade, Editorial Assistant, P. O. Box 1120, Glendora, CA 91740. (626) 335-8069. FAX: (626) 335-6127. E-mail: <dottie@walters-intl.com> or <www.walters-intl.com>

Another contact is *Market Yourself As a Speaker* by Susan Levin. This comb-bound book addresses creativity that matches you and the organization that's looking for the right speaker.

Maybe your forte is as a lecturer, trainer, educator. *Career Track* trains more than 750,000 people each year throughout the world. It offers seminars on every topic imaginable. Being an author is a plus. To apply as a trainer, call (303) 447-2323, ext 2559 and listen to the recorded message on becoming a media trainer. Then submit a training video shot of you in front of a live audience, a resume or press kit, and a list of topics you're an expert on. Contact the Trainer Recruiter, Mail Stop 15, 3085 Center Green Drive, Boulder, CO 80301-5408. (303) 440-7440. FAX: (303) 442-0392. E-mail: <shop@careertrack.com> or <www.careertrack.com>

That wasn't so hard. Now let's get all your tools together in Chapter Three.

3

It's Tool Time

If you're talking with another author and writing your name and address on scraps of paper as your business introduction, let's introduce you to a number of products that will bring you into the 21st Century. Below is a inventory of writing tools the ideal office should have. Cost factors may place some items on your wish list for a later date. The key is to prioritize what you must have now to be professional, and what you can farm out, like printing and copying services.

Business Cards

Don't scrimp on budget dollars when it comes to stationery and business cards. Scraps of paper, the back of a deposit slip, or worse yet, the back of someone else's business card is not the professional way to network. It isn't advisable to pour out the contents of a purse or take everything out of the wallet that has been smashed in your rear pocket, in search of a card. Keep them in a small briefcase, the conference tote, or a cardholder—fresh, crisp, not bent or dingy.

Software makes creating business cards, brochures and letterheads a snap. Paper Direct is one source. Call (800) 272-7377 for their free catalog.

And don't print too many at a time. Zip codes change. So do area codes. Don't cross out old numbers. Opt instead to make fresh, new cards and stationery.

Never leave home without them. They're especially important at book signings, conventions, conferences and seminars. Exchange them with the world.

When you give one away, get one in return. Those cards are the building blocks of potential fans and/or clients. Networking builds mailing lists. That person may also have special training that will assist you in writing. Every card is a source for some marketing portion of your career.

Send a card out in all first-time correspondence, including paying bills. Leave one on restaurant dining tables with your tip, and put one in the counter jars for free lunch drawings. Get to know your locals. You need name recognition.

Should they be fancy or plain? Colored card stock or iridescent material? Professional? Or computer generated?

Harlan Ellison's card states simply, "I write."

Raul Melendez has the name of his debut novel, *Mercy Street*, on the front of his card and a brief synopsis of the story on the back.

Lawrence Block's card bears no mention that he's a prolific mystery author, teacher and mentor. Only his name, address, phone and FAX number, in black ink, appears on a pure white card.

Thom Racina has a black linen card with white ink, giving us addresses in both Palm Springs, California, and Washington, D.C.

ATTORNEY AT LAW Joseph Fleischmann II. has a marbleized pink and cream-colored card.

Marcia Talley puts her book jacket photo on the left side of the card. The title, *Sing it to Her Bones* is at the top, followed by the name of her series. The balance of her card contains information on how to contact her.

The point here is: be creative. You are the writer. Your business card is an extension of you.

Private box number

There are a lot of strange people out there. Not your fans, of course, but others. Insulate yourself and protect your home privacy with a postal box. You can rent from the post office or one of the many commercial postal services located in neighborhood shopping centers near you.

The post office box is inexpensive at about $20 a year. Commercial company prices vary from $40 to $110 annually. If you use a postal service, select a private one that doesn't charge premiums on postage or packaging. Many do. And don't rent the largest box. Both places will leave you a blue "you have a big item" slip when your box fills with royalty checks. Best of all, the rental expense is tax deductible against your earnings.

And while you're on tour, both will collect your mail so it doesn't pile up at home.

Telephone

Answer professionally, even if it is your home phone. On the answering machine, leave a warm, creative message. And update often. Don't talk about the snowfall when it's summertime. Abruptness or some old cliche, "This is an answering machine, you know what to do," will get you the desired result. They will hang up. This is a marketing tool. Develop a positive message. Draw the caller into your realm. Want them to beg to speak with you, after all, they found your special and probably unlisted telephone number. And you're going to be a famous author.

Whenever possible, answer the telephone yourself. Don't ask anyone to "Pound One" to leave a message for you.

In *The Excellence Challenge*, author Tom Peters says, "The only magic of the $40 billion giant IBM is that in a $500 billion industry they happen to be the only company that still answers the phone."

1-800 or 1-888 Numbers

If the direct mail concept works for your product, these toll-free services that connect you to your customer base are a must. To achieve the best return for this expense, you must accept credit cards, and should have a 24-hour day, 7-day week answering service. To check on current rates call:

- AT&T (800) 222-0400
- LDDS Communications (800) 737-8423
- MCI Telecommunications (800) 777-1099
- Telecom MCI (800) 866-3322
- US Sprint (800) 366-1046

For those of you who don't expect a high volume of calls, maybe a toll-free answering service fits your criteria. A current list can be found *The Complete Direct Marketing Sourcebook*.

Press Kits and Photos

The press kit is the most important tool you have as a writer. As you develop into a professional writer, lecturer, and teacher, this tool will undergo many changes. Allow for flexibility. You'll need photographs and several enclosures. Let's start with the pictures.

Color or black and white? As Dallas Cowboy Deion Sanders says, "Both."

This is another area you cannot skimp on the budget funds. Contact local photographers and get bids. The photographer for your newspaper may be an independent contractor who knows exactly what you need and when you need it. Pay a deposit only, not the entire session fee, until you get an opportunity to view the photos and negatives.

Negotiate for the proofs and/or the opportunity to print in greater quantity later. You own the negatives. When you need to reorder, take them to a less expensive developer for reprints. The black-and-white glossy photo is a must for newsletters and newspapers. It's the real person you are, the one that will appeal to the media.

Don't try tricky poses or place your hands or other objects next to your face. The newspapers often "crop" pictures to fit the width of the columns and the length of the space. When cut to size, the hand may look as if it belongs to someone who isn't in the picture.

If you wear glasses, find a pair of empty frames similar to the ones you usually wear. This reduces glare. The camera needs to photograph your eyes, not the lens.

Ask the photographer for 5 x 7's or 3 x 4's. They are cheaper to develop and easier to let go of. The newspaper will not normally return the photograph. If you're local, they should have a "morgue," or library of photos, and will save yours for future use. If you must have the photo back, include a SASE with a request.

There's no photographer talented enough to make you younger, thinner, or less wrinkled. Miracles only happen in the movies. But you should expect a clear, good portrait that is flexible enough to meet all your needs.

After you've gone to all this trouble, don't get your feelings hurt if the article is published without your photo. It's a matter of time and space. Nothing personal.

HINT: I went to a glamour shot store at the local mall with my gun (after getting permission from the mall owner, of course) and did a major "big hair and lots of sexy makeup" color shot for both my press kit and the book jacket. Total cost $75.

The black-and-white in a more formal studio ran $250, but I own the proofs and the opportunity to print more copies at a future date for a reduced price.

Be imaginative here. If your book is about animals, take the shot with your animal or better yet, photograph the animal alone. You can create mystique by not showing your photo at all on the jacket. The strength of a photo can turn them on, or off. It will generate interest to get you read, or negatively tossed in the trash can. It's that important.

For your first book, link your photo to the theme or book topic. You're defining not only your creative style throughout the tour, but your life as a writer, as well.

Buy bright, flat, not glossy 9" x 12" pocket folders from the local office supply store. Jewel-toned red, blue and green are particularly popular colors. Put your card in the slot on the left hand side and your photo in the pocket behind that.

Enclose any value-added marketing item you've developed.

HINT: I slip one of my book markers and a postcard that has my book jacket cover on it in front of the photo.

On the right hand side place the following in order:
- (1) a fact sheet has the title, author name, publisher, number of pages, ISBN number, publication date, binding and price in both the United State and Canada
- (2) a synopsis (or excerpts) of the book, one or two pages in length
- (3) a one page author bio
- (4) press releases tied to current "hot" news
- (5) newspaper clippings
- (6) book quotes from reviewers and/or other readers
- (7) if the tour has been partially scheduled, include the itinerary to enhance the value of your presentation
- (8) prepare a list of twenty questions that an interviewer from television, radio or magazines might ask. Provide the answers too. Make them direct, funny, sharp, and crisp. This will help the host, who may not already know you, and will jumpstart your interview. If they haven't read the book yet, it will help them seem more informed and less embarrassed.

When you first build this kit, you'll have very little in the way of press releases, clips, or quotes. You may start with a "thank you" letter from a book signing event, and/or a quote from someone in the genre who loved the book. Quotes and testimonials from amateurs will also work for the first time kit. Use large fonts to make those few fill an entire page for volume.

These items will be discarded later in favor of professional reviews from *Publishers Weekly, Kirkus Review* and *Library Journal*. And from fans who'll e-mail you and/or place their review of the book on Amazon.com or Barnes & Noble.com.

A complete list of quotes is an important part of the press kit. Type them on one sheet, with the most powerful and visible at the top.

You may wish to include published articles that relate to your product. This reinforces that you are the expert on this topic.

Some authors include a copy of the book jacket. You should ask the publisher for the overprints anyway. A hundred or so is not an unreasonable request. If it's a hardback, carry extras to the book stores and replace those that have been damaged.

These kits must also be "modular" in form. Allow the flexibility to reach specific audiences. If you want to be a speaker or on a panels, focus on your speaking credits. If your repertoire includes other venues, like your career, a sheet profiling your expertise will achieve the best result.

Letterheads and envelopes for your stationery
Your manuscript is done in courier type, 12 point, on white bond paper. That is a professional style that works well for your

stationery as well. Other variations define you as an amateur. And, even if you are, don't tell anyone. Envelopes are #10 size. As in your selection of material for your business cards, the paper defines you. If you're the iridescent pink and silver type with butterflies—go for it.

Zip Code Book and Postal Scale

With the mobility of our population, regional changes throughout the United States occur often. Twenty to thirty percent of the addresses on your mailing list will change every year. A zip code book is critical in the care and maintenance of your mailing list, not to mention that accuracy expedites your correspondence.

While the list will be cleaned periodically, having the new codes expedite this tedious work. Software from sources like My Mail List is a writer's boon. This is a product of My Software Company, 1259 El Camino Real, Suite 167, Menlo Park, CA 94025; (800) 325-3508. In California (415) 325-9383. Call for a free catalog.

The postal scale is an inexpensive purchase. When you conduct a mass mailing, concentrate on the size and weight of the items to be mailed for cost efficiency. There's nothing more embarrassing than to send out correspondence and not have sufficient postage.

Bulk Mail

If you have less than 200 pieces for Standard Mail, or 500 pieces for First Class to be mailed at the same time, bulk mail maybe the less expensive way.

The keys to saving money are:
- Getting the mail the right size and shape for the post

office to process it
- Printing your addresses so they can be scanned by an optical character reader or barcode sorter
- Presorting the mail by ZIP Code
- Grouping the mail into packages in certain numbers
- Placing the packages into trays or sacks provided by the post office
- Delivering it to the post office. They don't offer home or office pick-up for bulk mail

My Software Company offers a simplified service on software from My Mail List. Web site:

<http://www.mysoftware.com/mailtips>

They also publish a guide called *The Basics of Bulk Mail*.

To learn more about bulk mail call (800) 275-8777. You'll need to ask for a permit application. There's a $100 annual fee.

Local U.S. Postal Service offices have copies of several publications that explain this procedure. You may call the USPS at (202) 783-3238 between 8 a.m. and 3:45 p.m. Eastern Standard Time and request a Domestic Mail Manual (also known as DMM). Or you may send a SASE to New Orders, Superintendent of Documents, U.S. Government Printing Office, P. O. Box 371954, Pittsburgh, PA 15250-7954. Home Page: <http://www.usps.gov>

Shipping Boxes and large envelopes

The mark of a well-informed, seasoned author who ships thick manuscripts will include the use of boxes:

- Box-in-a-Box Manuscript Sets at FHP, P. O. Box 106, Virginia Beach, VA 23450. (877) 427-0220. Online orders: <http://dragonet.com/writers>

- Papyrus Papers is located at 2216 Dundee Road, Louisville, Kentucky, 40205, (502) 451-9748, FAX: (502) 451-5487. E-mail: <info@papyrusplace.com> or <http://www.papyrusplace.com>
- Ship-it, 3600 Eagle Way, Twinsburg, Ohio 44087-2380. (800) 481 3600. FAX: (800) 525 6001. <www.shipitcatalog.co>

When shipping your manuscript, place stamps on the inside box with your return address on that box. The outside box can be canceled with a postal meter, but stamps are a must on the inside one.

If you prefer envelopes to boxes, compare postal rates. Depending on the number of pages being mailed, the postage for the box is often less expensive. Book rates for boxes simply costs less money.

Calendars

Make a calendar for you, the publicist, your agent, and your family. They should all conform with dates, including family blackout times for vacation and life. You do have a life, you know. Enter everything in pencil. You will have to change dates and make sure every person is notified of those changes to avoid double booking.

Computer and printer

Buy what you can afford to have and maintain it. The computer software capability is as important or more important than the computer and should drive what you buy. Whether you invest in a major IBM product, buy mail order through a computer warehouse, or inherit a used computer and printer, strive for top computer speed and memory.

HINT: Because of the number of projects I'm working on at any given time, I have installed Dragon Systems' Naturally Speaking and dictate much of my work. Dan Poynter in his *Write and Grow Rich* book explains this program best.

Use a high resolution laser printer. No professional writer uses dot matrix anymore. The manuscript paper is clear, white, bond. Fancy papers or colors clearly define you as an amateur, not as a maverick. To advance your writing career, this is an area where you want to fit in quietly.

FAX machine

It is predicted that within the next ten years, 75% of all business-to-business transactions will be via the FAX. Technology has already substituted the FAX for the telex.

When you need to proof documents, send out part of your press kit to a prospective client, or speak with someone in another time zone and who's difficult to reach, its speed makes this piece of office equipment a must.

If the FAX is built into your personal computer, all the better. It saves both time and paper.

The Official Facsimile Users' Directory lists over 30,000 FAX numbers. The *FAX Phone Book* has almost 200,000 additional numbers. Add your name to those directories. Others include:

- Bowker's Book Trade Fax & Phone Directory in paperback
- Kovels' Yellow Pages, published by Three Rivers Press
- University & College Phone Book, Stanley Alpern Editor

Label maker

No author can live without a label maker. It saves hours no writer can afford to waste. Make sure your software has the capacity to sort in zip code order.

- NEBS Inc offers the maker and software. Contact them at 500 Main Street, Groton, MA 01471, (800) 225-6380 or order online: <www.nebs.com>
- Seiko Instruments offers several makers and the software to manage it. Contact them at 1130 Ringwood Court, San Jose, CA 95131.(800) 688-0817

HINT: I started a mailing list with family, close friends, and clients from my former working life. Everyplace I go, I exchange cards with fans, writers, promoters, book store owners, people in line at the bank, the grocery, the airport—everywhere. That inner circle of names, now in excess of 2,700, has become the most important part of my promotional dowry. These people get advance notice if I'm speaking in their area, when a new book comes out, or if I'm going to be on television or radio in their city.

Don't forget these people at Christmas. It's not only a

way of thanking them for being a part of your life, but it washes the list for address accuracy.

Join writing groups. They have mailing lists. Obtain a list of key media contacts, both locally and through the *Literary Market Place*. Join social, volunteer, church, and/or fraternal organizations. See how the names and address list multiplies beyond your inner circle.

Buy association mailing lists that cover a broad range of topics. Contact Association List Company, 209 Madison Street, Alexandria, VA 22314-1764. (800) 899-4420. FAX on demand: (800) 496-4568. E-mail: <listinfo@marketinggeneral.com> or <www.mgi-net.com/mgilists>

Goodies, T-shirts, mugs, tote bags, etc.

T-shirts are walking billboards: expressive and individual. They're inexpensive marketing tools for raffles, gift baskets, presents, and conferences.

Try Creative Compression Packaging at (800) 678-7660 or their Web site <www.t-shirtpostcard.com> Their T-shirts are folded into postcard shapes, ready for mailing.

HINT: During a slow book signing night at a Texas mall, my husband found a kiosk that silk-screened T-shirts. He gave them a copy of my book and had T-shirts made up for several fans. Very inexpensive and clever. My husband wore one as he walked up and down the mall dragging buyers into the book store where I was signing.

99

For postcards, business cards, address labels or bookmarks, check for local printers. Sometimes the expense and time factor are important. For others compare prices by shopping with organizations like Premier Marketing Public Relations, Judy Waggoner, 2520 Crestview Drive, Appleton, WI 54915-3065. (920) 991-2614. FAX: (920) 991-2615.

Mugs and tote bags can also be silk-screened. These items are expensive because they must be purchased in volume. There usually isn't a decent price break until an order reaches 5,000 items.

As an alternative, use the camera-ready artwork from your zip disk and save a lot of money. Better yet, drop by the local arts and crafts store and buy the totes. They comes in several colors and fabrics. Create your own with stencils, patterns or other materials.

Try buttons, caps, magnets, key-chains or T-shirts that say, "Ask me about my ISBN number." Or "Have you read my book?" will catch some eyes. How about, "I'm a writer. For me, this is dressed up." These make wonderful "point-of-purchase" items at the book store cash register and/or stuffer gifts for the convention tote bags.

Bumper stickers and license plate frames are great visuals when you're on the road. The swap meet near your home will customize them with your message quite inexpensively.

HINT: I did bookmarks. Thirty-five hundred should cost less than $400. Mine are bright yellow with black letters. On one side it reads: POLICE LINE—DO NOT CROSS. On the other, in addition to the book title is the ISBN number, the Publishers name, and the web site address. I had them UV coated so they'd be sturdy and last longer. People love them. I give those away to strangers everywhere I travel.

Flyers and Brochures

Computer software has made this important tool incredibly easy to modify and maintain. Create them for press kits and individual mailings. They are a must for the speaker bureaus who will hire you. Use four-color, glossy paper on the front side with your photo and several bullets about your presentation. Use black-and-white on the back side listing all the organizations and places you've spoken.

These can be done on a home computer using a software program. Each presentation will have a different topic. And as your experiences grows, so does the list of your clients. Flexibility is the key to keeping this important tool current.

Access to a central library

A great deal of information for the writer is available in the library, including the oft times referred to: *Literary Market Place (LMP)*. Libraries can't afford current year editions, but the *LMP* is now online. When you are looking for a source, you will be contacting the resource direct to verify they're still in business, the address is correct, and the editor is the person who will review your project.

Credit Cards

If direct mail is a good source for selling your product, apply to all major credit cards. Not every customer will want to use cash, checks, or money orders. This country runs on credit. Contact your bank and ask for VISA and MasterCard application forms. You are "seeking credit card merchant status."

For others:

American Express - (800) 528-5200 on the mainland.
It's (800) 528-4800 for Hawaii and Alaska.

Carte Blanche - (800) 525-7376

Diner's Club - (800) 525-7376

Sear's Discover Card - (800) 322-4566

Web site

In this electronic age, the importance of the Internet and the role it plays in your success has a chapter all its own. (See Chapter Nine.) But as a tool, you should know that a web site is an extension of your press kit. Check out other writer's and Publisher's web sites. What do you like? What doesn't work for you? How can your site represent your product in it's highest form? This is a very inexpensive advertising item that keeps you and your fans in touch.

HINT: Mine, <http://members.aol.com/jspizer> contains a current personal message, a photo and book jacket cover, my appearance schedule, quotes from fans, links to other sites and most important of all, my e-mail address. Talk about shameless promotion.

E-mail

E-mail is the ultimate tool for the millennium. Every 24 hours, more than 30 million people in America use e-mail. It keeps your fans in touch, yet maintains your privacy. This address goes on the business card, the letterhead, and in the press kit. List it in organizational directories and on your web site.

It's now time to get organized.

4

Get Organized

This chapter is not about organizing your work. Book selling is a marketing war. Marketing is about finding, nurturing, and maintaining relationships. People want value. Offer them more than they expect. Join organizations. Lots of them.

Why? Because writing is a solitary, insular business. Organizational memberships provide a variety of benefits.

Writing organizations create networks, have conferences, print newsletters, sell advertising, and offer opportunities to showcase your talent. Genre groups like Romance Writers of America and Sisters-in-Crime are outstanding examples of those that showcase members' work.

Education, information and up-to-date pulse readings on America's ever changing publishing industry are major pluses to membership.

If you self-published, join the king. Publishers Marketing Association is the largest trade association where networking and learning are keys to your success. You can reach them on the Internet at <LISTSERV@hslc.org>

On a smaller scale, join SPAN, the Small Publishers Association of North America. Box 1306, Buena Vista, CO 81211-1306-1306.

HINT: I belong to eighteen organizations; fourteen of them are professional writing groups. Why would I involve myself in so many when I need to write? How did I select the organizations? How can they help my project? Read on.

If marketing is war, then put on your armor. Join organizations. Why? Consider the following reasons.

They offer a strong sense of satisfaction and define you as the person you are. Networking and bonding with other writers offer encouragement. You'll receive expert assistance from professionals, find educational resources and up-to-date information in your field.

If you're self-published, joining increases purchasing clout and exposure to those you wouldn't otherwise meet. Learn from them.

A few organizations provide reasonably priced medical and dental benefits. There may be opportunities for your freelance work that also bring recognition to your bigger picture–the novel.

Some groups offer critique services. Others will advise you regarding literary agency and agents. While others may provide mentoring programs. Local chapters maintain audio and video tape libraries of speakers and many hold competitions, offer awards, have monthly local meetings, and annual national conventions.

The Austin Writers' League is an all-genre full service organization. They help writers promote and sell their work. They provide resources, publications, educational opportunities, media exposure, special events and networking. AWL also rents out their 1,600 member **mailing list**. They produce a monthly thirty-minute radio program, *Writing on the Air*, on Austin's KOOP Radio. And from September through May, writers are featured on the *Mid-Day Bookshelf*, a TV segment that airs on KVUE-TV.

The National Writer's Association is another all-genre organization. They are located at 3140 South Peoria, Suite 295, Aurora, CO 80014. Contact them at (303) 841-0246 or FAX: (303) 751-8593. Chapters meet monthly throughout the United States. Networking, information, and addressing the needs of the local writers are their main objectives. NWA offers critique services, freelance opportunities in their *Authorship Magazine*, agent recommendations, contests, award programs and conventions. Their online service promotes the author's product, including links to web sites.

Romance Writers of America is located at 3707 FM 1960 West, Suite 550, Houston, Texas 77068. Don't think of Danielle Steele and romance. This genre includes exotic alternatives to the "bosom rippers" you've heard about. Think: mystery, cozy, historical, western, intrigue, inspirational, contemporary, mainstream, time travel, new age and paranormal.

Sisters-in-Crime's world headquarters can be contacted at P. O. Box 442124, Lawrence, KS 66044; (785) 842-1325. FAX: (785) 842-1034. E-mail: <sistersincrime@juno.com> This international group of "sisters" includes many "brothers." If you're a mystery fan, pre-published or published author, this is the organization for you.

Organizations you select should have:
- Magazines and newsletters that offer "how-to" articles
- Opportunities for you to contribute writing of your own
- Editing and critique services
- Monthly local meetings where you network with other writers, meet professional instructors and experts in all fields
- Kudo pages where you tout your new novel and the tour
- A mailing list and host an annual and/or regional conference.

It's your job not to nitpick, but to network. In networking you can't imagine how many strange, wonderful, and funny people you will meet. Some will become lifelong friends. Others will remain fellow writers. You may find a publicist, a lawyer, or an accountant who will become a character in one of your future novels.

Or you may fulfil your need to volunteer and help others. Whatever your reason, join.

Remember the most important tool to selling your novel is finding buyers. Your mailing list is your dowry, what you bring to the publishing table.

HINT: Imagine the raised eyebrows when I mention my mailing list contains over 2,700 names. That number does not include the organizational membership lists. Remember, you only need to sell 15,000 hardback copies of your book to reach the best seller List. Start that mailing list today. Give a card. Get a card.

99

Many of these organizations offer monthly meetings and have fascinating and educational speakers in the fields of law enforcement, forensics, medical and legal, and other experts. These people become resources for information you may need later in your writing. You'll find many friends in these "like" groups. They also open doors for speaking opportunities if you have a special field of expertise.

Writing organizations, both national and local, have magazines and newsletters. This media broadens the audience for your freelance work, an announcement regarding your new book, or an ad outlining your scheduled tour.

They may teach you how to negotiate a contract, sell short stories you've written, or write freelance articles.

Attend writing conferences. Local, state, regional, national, and worldwide conferences are all very important extensions of your success. They **educate**, create visibility for you, and help you develop name recognition. You'll meet new friends, sit on panels, conduct book signings, and meet lots of famous writers.

Don't forget the speaker bureaus. This is an untapped market resource for many writers. If you have an expertise or specialty career, develop a variety of different programs and pitch yourself on the talk circuit. They pay very well and you sell books.

Join several professional speaker bureaus or create your own. For someone who has written a book and has a repertoire of programs, they can command speaking fees ranging from

$750 to $2,000. Whether you live in a resort area, a metropolitan city, or a small community, don't miss a fabulous opportunity to meet people from around the world who **attend conferences** and conventions. And buy books.

Check the local Yellow Pages and the Internet for **Speaker Bureaus** in your area. You may not command fees like former President George Bush of $84,000, but the honorarium pays bills, helps you perfect your author persona and "sound bytes" and boosts you into the realm of the "recognized."

Several national bureaus include:

- Dottie Walters Speaker Services at P. O. Box 398, Glendora, CA 91740; (626) 335-8069, FAX: (626) 335-6127. Dottie teaches and schedules speakers. Her international magazine, *Sharing Ideas*, offers major exposure to the writer/speaker

- Multimedia Publishing and Packaging, Inc, 9430 Topanga Canyon Blvd, Suite 200, Chatsworth, CA 91311; (800) 982-8138. Wonder how the "big guys" do it? From design to packaging, this is the organization that professionalizes their speaking materials.

- Speakers Platform at <www.speaking.com> showcases speakers and trainers for the international market. Contact them at P. O. Box 21631, Santa Barbara, CA 93121; (800) 220-6232, FAX: (805) 965-6522. E-Mail: <Speakers@speaking.com>

- Tu-Vets Printing for full color flyers from 1,250 to 20,000 copies. Contact them at 5635 E. Beverly Blvd, Los Angeles, CA 90022; (323) 723-4569. Outside California (800) 894-8977, FAX: (323) 724-1896

- Embassy Media for audio, video, and CD duplication, and accessories. Contact them at (800) 593-5757. Home

Page: <www.embassymedia.com>
- Cassette Works for audio and video duplication. Call or write for a free service kit at 125 N. Aspan Avenue, Azusa, CA 91742; (800) 423-TAPE
- Speakers for Free is a bi-monthly publication with a 30,000 circulation to showcase you as a speaker. Contact Susan Levin at (310) 822-4922, FAX: (310) 822-9025. E-mail: <susan@speakerservices.com> or <http://speakerservices.com>
- Western Association News is an independent magazine for associations. If your product and knowledge matches specific groups or if you're looking for meeting planners, contact them at 13274 Fiji Way, Fourth Floor, Marina del Rey, CA 90292; (310) 577-2700, FAX: (310) 577-3715

Remember, you're **developing resources** to help you write your second novel and promote you and your book. Along the way you'll meet experts in fields that may come in handy for a future project. Need an anthropologist? How about a family therapist? Maybe a retired FBI agent? They're out there waiting to help you.

No book signing or speech is too small or unimportant unless distance or expense is an issue.

HINT: I spoke at a local library before twenty people. A young Brit asked a lot of questions, but left without buying a book. I sold six books that day. However, that young man e-mailed me later and offered me an opportunity to speak at a major

book store. So far that gig led to seven more book signings.
And the book sales now exceed four hundred.

99

If you are the expert in your field, help others find you with
these helpful hints:

- If your product dictates, advertise in card packs
- Add a page in the very back of the book, offering a
  discount coupon for the purchase of a future book, or
  another copy of that book, or rebate for volume
  purchasing
- Request they contact you by e-mail and/or your 1-800
  number for speaking engagements
- Autograph your book and donate them for auctions and
  raffles. Decorate baskets that include the novel. If your
  book is a love story add a soft background music tape,
  candles, and sparkling water

Libraries are organizations too. They have a budget and buy
books, especially from local authors. They also offer reading
programs where you can speak and sell to the public.

R.R. Bowker Company will rent library mailing lists, if
you specifically request genre information. The address is 121
Chanlon Road, New Providence, New Jersey 07974; (908) 464-
6800, FAX: (908) 508-7696. E-mail: <info@bowker.com> or
<http://www.bowker.com>

Some major regional library systems are:

- Atlanta Public Library, One Margaret Mitchell Square
  NW., Atlanta, GA 30303-1089, (404) 982-3560
- Buffalo & Erie County Public Library System, Lafayette

Square, Buffalo, New York 19203-1887, (716) 858-8900, FAX: (716) 858-1211
- Chicago Public Library, Harold Washington Library Center, 400 South State Street, Chicago, IL 60605, (312) 747-4999 or 747-4300, FAX: (312) 747-4962
- Dallas Public Library, 1515 Young Street, Dallas, Texas 75201-5499, (214) 670-1400, FAX: (214) 670-7839
- Denver Public Library, 10 West 14th Avenue Parkway, Denver, CO 80204-2749, (303) 640-6200 or 640-6146, FAX: (303) 640-6143
- Free Library of Philadelphia, 919 Walnut Street, Philadelphia, PA 19107-5289, (215) 683-3213 or (800) 222-1754, FAX: (215) 683-3211
- Hawaii State Library, Contact them at 478 South King Street, Honolulu, Hawaii 96813, (808) 586-3553
- Houston Public Library, 500 McKinney Avenue, Houston, Texas 77002-2534, (713) 247-1925
- Los Angeles Public Library, 630 West Fifth Street, Los Angeles, CA 90071-2097, (213) 228-7515, FAX: (213) 228-7429
- Miami-Dade Public Library System, 101 W. Fagler Street, Miami, Fla 33130-1523, (305) 375-2665, FAX: (305) 372-6428
- Multnomah County Library, 205 East Russell, Portland, OR 97212, (503) 248-5402, FAX: (503) 248-5441
- New York Public Library, 188 Madison Avenue, New York, New 10016, (212) 930-0800, FAX: (212) 921-2546
- Ogdensburg Public Library, 312 Washington Street, Ogdensburg, New York 13669, (315) 393-4325
- Rocky River Public Library, 1600 Hampton Road,

Rocky River, OH 44116
- Salt Lake City Library System, 209 East 500 South, Salt Lake City, UT 84111, (801) 524-8200, FAX: (801) 524-8272
- San Diego County Library, 555 Overland Avenue, Building 15, San Diego, CA 92123, (619) 694-2414, FAX: (619) 495-5981
- San Francisco Public Library, 100 Larkin Street, San Francisco, CA 94102-9734, (415) 557-4400 or 557-4277, FAX: (415) 557-4239
- Seattle Public Library, 1000 Fourth Avenue, Seattle, Wash 98104-1193, (206) 386-4636, FAX: (206) 386-4108

And don't forget the largest organization of them all, our "men and women in uniform." This is an untapped resource for sales. At any given time, the United States government has more than one million personnel in the armed forces stationed all over the world. They read books and they buy from the PX. But, as you might suspect, selling to the government is an art.

Write the Superintendent of Documents, U.S. Government Printing Office, Washington, D.C. 20402, (202) 783-3238 and request a publication called Selling to the Military, #008-000-479-0. This will cost about $10.00.

For the charitable organizations in your life, designate a charity to receive a portion of your net proceeds. This can be announced on the acknowledgment page of your book, the author's note, on a separate flyer, a poster, or at a special event for that charity.

Now that you're organized, have the physical and speaking tools, let's move those books.

5

Who, when and how to "book 'em"

What about the tour? Jacqueline Susann may have been the creator of the celebrity/author tour when she promoted *Valley of the Dolls* in 1966. But for the rest of us, book signing tours began in the 1980's at a time when independent book stores made up more than 50% of the book selling market. Remember those days before the major chains? The mega stores? The coffee and soft comfortable chairs? Before Amazon.com and Barnes & Noble.com?

Terry McMillan thumped and stumped promoting her first novel, *Mama*. By the time *Waiting to Exhale* was published, the booksellers approached her.

Is the mega book tour dead? Elaine Petrocelli, with Book Passage in Corte Madera says, "We have events at 8 a.m. that are so big we have to rent the theater next door."

Algonquin Publishing of Chapel Hill, North Carolina, employed a unique tactic to promote Ann Mariah Cook's *Running North*. Reported in *Publishers Weekly (PW)*, on March

15, 1999, they sent Ms. Cook, an accomplished dog sledder, along with several other dog-sled teams through the snow on book tour between New Hampshire bookstores. They served hot chocolate and pastries, and video taped the event. The signings made national news and, most importantly, they sold all the books in stock in both stores.

Imagine Anne Rice on a three month bus book tour in 1995, during which time she also wrote a travel diary for an online magazine. She combined her bookstore appearances with blood drives in many cities. After all, she knows vampires. Those who gave blood were given a button that read, "I gave blood to the Vampire Armand," and they jumped to the head of her book signing table as their reward. If you ever stood in line for Anne's autograph, you know what a great perk that was.

Courageous mystery writers, Martin J. Smith and Philip Reed, piled their kids into a minivan and toured the country together during one four week, ten-state summer odyssey. They took this trip without their wives.

In 1992, Sarah Weeks committed to a forty city tour to launch her debut novel and cassette package, *Crocodile Smith*. She carried a karaoke player, which at the time was not as well known as it is today.

In the "you shoulda' been there" department, Patricia Cornwell, who earned her helicopter pilot's license, bought a 'copter after having a Scarpetta logo emblazoned on its side. On August 7, 1999, she piloted solo and landed in the parking lot of a major book chain in her hometown of Richmond, Virginia.

Kevin J. Anderson, author of 25 novels including *Ai! Pedrito!*, holds the Guinness World Record for the "largest single-author book signing in history," signing thousands of hardcover copies on July 3, 1998 at a major chain in Los

Angeles. That year's tour included 40 scheduled appearances, 27 cities in 28 days, both in the United States and Canada. He's also the first fiction author in history to sign at the Target Department Store chain. If his name isn't familiar to you, you're not a *X-File*, *Star Wars* or sci-fi fan.

According to *Publishers Weekly*, Borders and Barnes & Noble schedule more than 23,000 events each year. The independents organize 400 more.

To unite and excite the changing reader, bookstores added warm fuzzy reading spaces, plush sofas and chairs, and cappuccino bars. They also hired customer service representatives (CSR) whose sole responsibility is the co-ordinated effort to bring authors and readers into their stores.

Daily calendars, large billboards touting the visiting author, multiple magazine and newspaper racks, music and computer software departments, creative writing classes, and programs devoted to genres like mystery or children, create a homey one-stop shopping environment that means more exposure for the author, and more income to the seller.

What about the tour? The book tour requires a flexible day job, disposable income (spending dollars you can goodbye to), a loving and supportive family, groups of close friends (some of them writers), an ego made of Kryptonite, a smile and strong handshake, frequent flyers miles you've saved for years, and a strong marketing savvy. You're not in this business to make money. You're an author.

HINT: Ray Bradbury told the story about his marriage to his beautiful wife, Maggie, very early in his writing career. He had placed a few dollar bills in an envelope and, after the wedding ceremony, handed the envelope to the minister.

The reverend said, "I heard you're a writer."

Ray answered, "Yes, I am."

The minister handed the unopened envelope back to Ray saying, "Then you're going to need this more than I do."

Most large publishing houses will only book a six to eight city tour for a mid-list author. Their marketing budget averages $1,200 per book. They claim it's the law of diminishing returns for them financially.

How do you find bookings?

In addition to the *Literary Market Place*, how do you find those stores that actively promote author signings?

- One source that has compiled a list of over 500 independent bookstores is Open Horizons, P. O. Box 205, Fairfield, IA 52556. (515) 472-6130 or (800) 796-6130. FAX: (515) 472-1560. E-mail: <info@bookmarket.com>

What about your financial returns? Remember in Chapter One we covered the basic questions of your business plan. They included:

- Who will buy the book?
- How do I position myself in the market to guarantee sales?
- How do I create a desire for this work?
- How do I sustain sales over a period of time?

When you position yourself in the market, you will make money. But it takes considerable time and effort on your part. Maximum exposure outside your local area is critical to hand-selling the book and creating name recognition. That's why you're doing the tour. Not for your first book, but those you'll write later.

Mid-list writers aren't going to get the big advance bucks, the dumps (those colorful cardboard stands advertising and holding your book), or the shelf space that Grisham and Koontz receive. You must be creative to enhance your share of the market sales, to meet your business goals. Here are ideas that work:

- Get someone in the store to read your book. Most stores have an eye-level "recommended reading" shelf that will boost sales
- When signing at an independent store, send them a poster for their window. When you leave after the event, offer to sign it for the store owner
- Ask to be situated toward the front of the book store, near the entrance or a high foot traffic area
- Even though you may have scheduled only an hour there, be prepared to stay until the last potential customer in your line has been greeted
- Become your own sales person
- When readers ask, and they will, "Who do you like to read?" have an author or their body of work in mind and answer readily.
- This helps the store sell additional titles
- After the signing, autograph as much of the leftover stock as the store suggests. They place stickers that read

"Signed Copy," or "Autographed First Editions," and place those in a special area in the store. Those books sell. Some distributors will not allow autographed books to be returned by the store, so consider those you signed—sold.

- If it's not a big chain who has their own printing department and makes professional posters in metal stands, provide the store with a photo of you and one of the front book jacket, or a poster you've produced.
- If it's a large store, provide duplicate signs to be strategically placed throughout the store.
- On the genre shelf turn at least one of your books "face out," a major plus because the cover is far more enviable than seeing the spine.
- In fact, when you go to any book store, whether you're there in an official capacity or not, "fix" your novel to achieve that look.
- On the signing table set one or more books upright.
- Carry several identical pens. If you've autographed them in black, the balance of the dedication and date, etc, needs to be in the same ink.
- If you're signing at a location other than a book store i.e., luncheon, conference, workshop, private home, designate someone to stand slightly behind you to accept the book, open it to the page you want to sign, and slide it under your hands. This gives you more time and freedom to talk with your buyer. You can look at your new fan and share more "chat" time rather than thumbing through the front of the book for the signing page.
- It's smoother and less distraction for you both.

- Always be prepared. Carry books every time you leave the house.
- Wear comfortable shoes. Standing authors greet potential customers.
- Know where the restrooms are. If you're sitting down, customers will inevitably mistake you for the store's information person.
- Carry a camera. Take photos of yourself and your store contact.
- Autograph and mail the photo with your "thank you" note. That'll be your invitation to speak next year.
- On your first tour wear a name tag. This defines you as the author, not the employee.

HINT: My first signing was Valentine's Day 1998, at an independent store. I baked heart shaped cookies. You know, those Betty Crocker packages that come in a roll? The four dozen fit nicely in a red, heart-shaped $.39 plastic bowl. Later, the book store owner recommended me for a paying job at the Learning Tree University. And she's still hand-selling the novel.

One often overlooked **non-traditional** book signing and selling market, especially for the mid-list author, is the library system. Many libraries have developed year-round programs designed to bring more readers into their realm. Be prepared to donate one or two books to the library's inventory as a goodwill gesture. And, while the "Friends of the Library" will sell your book, expect to bring the books you will sell. Negotiate in advance what percentage of the sale you'll donate to the "Friends." Sixty for you and forty for the house is not unusual.

Mail them your press kit just as you would to a book store. If the library is near, drop off a poster they can use in the lobby to announce your attendance.

HINT: Using a software program, I created book marks announcing the library program, included mailing labels for the area zip code from my master list, and delivered them. The librarian was pleasantly surprised with this idea. They gave a book mark to everyone who rented a book and seemed interested in the program.

Using our combined mailing lists, the library mailed more book marks, wrote a nice news release for the newspaper, and a reporter covered the event, which resulted in a front page article and photo afterward. The librarian thought the idea so unique, she reimbursed me the paper costs and now announces many of her programs in this manner. Where else can you buy advertising that cheap?

Book distributor Baker and Taylor has published state-by-state directories of libraries that offer author readings. This reference includes the library name, location, contact information and areas of interest. Contact the library marketing division at Baker and Taylor, 652 East Main Street, P. O. Box 734, Bridgewater, New Jersey 08807-0920; (908) 218-0400 for a copy.

Many corporations and organizations will often pass on authors unless the event can benefit you and their store. In today's market, it's all bottom-line for everyone concerned in selling. Before scheduling the tour, consider these questions and have ready answers:

- Develop a sales pitch.
- Can you sell books?
- What's your "sound byte?"
- What is your dowry?
- Do you have a large area mailing list?
- Is this your home town?
- Can you and/or your publisher co-op a press release and advertising to bring readers into the store?
- Can you position yourself with a value-added promotion?
- Can you teach their creative writing class?
- Can you turn your product into a fund raiser?
- Can you develop a panel and bring in other authors in your genre?
- Do you know people with complimentary products?
- Look to specialty groups according to their interests, careers, sex, lifestyle, race, creed or political beliefs, if that will work with your product and your message.

A select number of large houses bring in the big authors and, rather than scheduling book tours, simply take the book buyers out to dinner with the author. The selling is left to the buyers. From the publishing standpoint, part of this is economics. Sometimes it's because the author can't speak in public, won't, or doesn't want to speak. How many top-ten "perennial" authors do you know who go on tour?

M. Scott Peck, author of *The Road Less Traveled* set a personal goal of one radio show a day as a critical part of his marketing plan. He conducted over 1,000 the first year, most from the comfort of his own home.

To locate some excellent radio interview shows order *Essential Radio Guide* from Peregrine Press, P. O. Box 363, Marblehead, MA 01945. (800) 299-2636. E-mail: <esntlradio@aol.com>

Events, whether major or minor, are part of the local outreach programs in every city. They bring readers into the stores. Don't be discouraged by the fact that more than forty million Americans over the age of eight cannot read and only one in seven of those numbers will ever enter a book store or library. Make it your responsibility to increase both literacy and readership.

Offer to present your book for book clubs. Churches, schools and private groups also conduct book reviews. And they buy books.

Should you speak at the chains or the independents? The answer is yes-to both. Many genres have specialty independent (indies) book stores. The advantages are obvious. They have a dedicated client base, are locally owned and operated, and the owners read and hand-sell your book, matching your genre to their readers.

HINT: Two independent book stores posted my debut novel on their best sellers list the summer of 1998. Their customers believe and trust that the owners will match their reading interests with a new author. One independent places so much confidence in their reading recommendation that they guarantee a full refund if the buyer isn't completely satisfied with the title suggestion. The faithful mystery fan is the best.

While the major chains are gobbling up the indies, you must support the indies. They welcome you into their cozy reading rooms, get to know who you are, friendships develop, and they continue to follow your career and recommend you for other speaking opportunities. They have mailing lists and do newsletters. More good stuff for your press kit.

The mystery genre is fortunate to have a wonderful resource.

The Deadly Directory contains a listing of all mystery book stores, conferences, awards, magazines and newsletters, collectors, Internet connections, fan clubs, mystery theater and party planners, and writer organization in the WORLD. They also offer all the listings on labels, and to enhance your mailing accuracy, they guarantee all those addresses. It's how they maintain up-to-date records in this ever-changing industry. *Deadly Serious Press* is located at 868 Arlington Avenue, Berkeley, CA 94707-1938. E-mail: <info@deadlyserious.com>

or <Http://www.deadlyserious.com> The cost
is less than forty dollars.

There are ways to **reduce your costs**. Before those dates are
scheduled, make sure the book signings have ultimate value to
you and to your fans. Ensure publicity, balloons, flyers, and
media attendance. Mail out postcards to all those names on your
mailing lists within three or four zip codes of the store location.

First class postcards are often less expensive to mail out
then bulk mail rates. And you get address corrections from
postcards free.

Make a second set of those labels and send them to the
book store for their newsletter mailing. Double and triple
whammy your sales.

Post your appearance schedule on your web site. Also
Authors on the Highway at 245 W. 17th St, 5th Floor, New
York, New York 10011, or <roadtrip@Bookwire.com> will
advertise your schedule. NOTE: Aimee Beckerman from this
organization is an excellent book reviewer. For guidelines
inquire at <aimee@Bookwire.com>

<Writersclub.com> hosts chat rooms where you can
plug the tour.

Post your schedule and/or link your web site to all
organizations you've joined.

Don't overlook the remote reader. BookTalk founder
David Knight found a market for this service, a 24-hour
recorded book-discussion line, for those readers who can't get
to signings. "It creates that bridge between the author and
reader." This is an excellent resource for your publisher/or
yourself to advertise your product. 1-818-788 9722 for more
information.

When you're visiting a new town for any reason, grab the phone directory and locate all the book stores. Always drop by, offer to sign books, meet and greet the (CSR) Customer Service Representatives who book authors. And, in the case of the indies, meet the owners. Those stores reap the benefits of having autographed books, without the expense of having you there. Again, more sold books. They must get to know you, because your success depends on it.

HINT: When I'm away from home, I always visit the local mystery stores. Sometimes I take cookies, a fresh press release, or offer to take the owners to lunch. Marketing is finding and nurturing long term relationships.

Develop "sound bytes" and create presentations that focus on a multitude of issues and concerns to local organizations like Rotary, Soroptmists, Kiwanis, Lions, Elks, Moose, and the Optimists. Join the Chamber of Commerce. They have a newsletter, hold weekly meetings and possess a large mailing list of local retailers who are potential booksellers and buyers. People who belong to one group often belong to more. Those contacts extend your speaking opportunities, your networking, and your mailing list.

Don't forget seminars on cruise lines. Negotiate and you may receive the cruise free or at least at a greatly reduced rate.

Going to a spa? Offer to speak in exchange for room and board. Massage therapists barter. So can you.

Introduce yourself to all the book buyers at K-Mart, Price Club (Costco), Sam's Club, and Wal-Mart, and work your way up the "food chain" to the regional purchaser for books. Locally, a few managers have purchasing power and most would welcome a non-traditional book signing. Ask, ask, ask. The hard work doesn't begin unless they say "no." The "yes" is easy. Remember that 53% of all books are sold through discount houses, price clubs, drug stores, and other non-bookstore climates.

Speaking of non-traditional markets, look for places where your book may be a hit:

- Off Highway? Try truck stops, convenience stores, car washes and dealerships.
- What about professional places, like medical offices, hospital gift shops, cafeterias, museums, specialty stores, local schools, greeting card shops, pet stores, churches, strip retail stores, and malls?
- In new technology there's QVC, Home Shopping Network, television infomercials, Internet writer's forums, and electronic bulletin boards.
- People who eat, buy books. Don't forget cafeterias, convenience stores, and restaurants.
- The world's on the move. Airline in-flight magazines, airport gift shops, car rental agencies, travel agencies, salons, and catalog sales. Take a book to the gift store at the hotel where you're staying. Find out who the buyers are and bombard them with your press.
- Find quiet places like libraries and coffee houses.
- Government agencies.
- Fun family events like street fairs, festivals, and trade shows. To reduce costs at these public events, try co-oping with someone else on the price of a booth.
- Banks and savings and loans.

- Auto clubs.
- The postal service where your mail box is located.
- Consider education a part of your contribution? Sponsor a community activity. Mentor a writing contest. Offer to teach classes in your field of expertise. Contact colleges and universities and propose to teach a class or be a "visiting" instructor. Call the Learning Annexes. Their pay is minimal, but the contacts and the potential for future work is ideal.
- Contact independent organizations that have banded together to form their own "brand." The Northern California Independent Booksellers Association, based in Corte Madera, California, represents almost 300 books stores throughout Northern California. The brand is "Book Sense." They have buying power and book signing is a one-stop shopping opportunity. Contact them at 5643 Paradise Drive, Suite 12, Corte Madera, CA 94925, (415) 927-3937, FAX: (415) 927-3971
- The American Booksellers Association, representing book stores throughout the United States, is another. Contact them at 828 South Broadway, Tarrytown, New York 10591, (914) 591-2665 or (800) 637-0037, FAX: (914) 591-2720. E-mail: <preynol@bookweb.org> or <http://www.bookweb.org>

These groups associate themselves with knowledge of their products, are passion about literacy, involvement in community, and personalities that meet reader needs and bond the reader to the author. What else would you need?

When you're on the tour and budget dollars concern you, consider these cost reduction ideas:

- Sharing rooms
- Getting reduced rates through AAA, AARP, etc.
- Using frequent flyer miles
- Staying with friends and family
- Calling airline brokers that buy blocks of seats at greatly reduced rates

Regardless of the Publisher's participation in your publicity program, you can do much on your own to increase your exposure. What better way to do this than a "free" story filler? This becomes part of your **publicity package**. After outlining the book tour, a simple, yet effective publicity method is the **Press Release**. You must have the answers to the following questions:

- When does the media want a press release?
- How should it look on paper?
- What information does the media want?
- What is the reader interested in?
- Can you solve a major problem?
- Can this release inform, inspire, entertain, or educate?
- What specific knowledge do you have above all others in your similar position?
- Where do I send it?
- How do I find the media sources?
- Do I need to hire a **clipping service**?

Let's face it, the media wants press releases because they need news. If you are announcing the release of your book, a speaking engagement in the area, an award you've won, a conference you're attending, a book signing, anywhere you want an audience, send out a press release.

A news release follows a standard format, is businesslike, double spaced, generally contains less than 850 words, and is typed on plain white bond paper.

Start at the top of the page, write NEWS RELEASE. A few lines down, type "For Immediate Release" followed by the date. Some publicists suggest this line begin at the far left; others start at the far right, so either is acceptable.

Drop down a couple more lines and type CONTACT: followed by your name and telephone number. Give daytime and evening numbers because presses run twenty-four hours a day. Add your address and e-mail too.

Drop several lines again and center a headline, preferably with an action verb: "Author wins Edgar Award." They may not use this headline, but it makes you look professional and gives the journalist an idea.

Now write the release. Double space your copy. The first paragraph contains all the basic information. It makes a statement, paints a pictures of the who, what, when, where, and why. The second paragraph is the solution. The third and last is the summary.

These can be reduced to several critical points:

- The *who*? Begin with your name . . .
- Followed by an active verb like "offers," "wins," "reveals"
- The *what* target market? Secrets, tips, alternatives, guidelines, advertises
- The *when*? The reader will reap benefits after they read it
- The *where and why*? Calls the reader to action
- Closing with a sharp, crisp ending.

Subsequent paragraphs add information. But the first paragraph may be the only thing that the newspaper, magazine, or radio station has time and space to use, so don't waste it.

At the end, type "End." A row of hash marks like ###### will also substitute as the ending.

The releases should be sent to daily and weekly newspapers, local magazines, news radio and television, including cable stations nearest the event. Send them at least two weeks in advance.

Don't overlook church bulletins, trade magazines, and all organizations you belong to. Many have newsletters and magazines that reach their entire membership list. Those press releases should be sent 60 days ahead of the event, as most of these are published monthly. When in doubt, call. You don't want to miss a printing deadline.

The first time you prepare a news release, you're going to find it time consuming. To identify the resources, the central library will have a reference section for sources like *Bacon's Magazine Directory, Bacon's Newspaper Directory,* and *Bacon's Newspaper and Television Directory.*

Write down the address and the editor's name and telephone number. Always call and verify the accuracy of all information printed anywhere. People are mobile in every industry. Writing is no exception.

You may wish to call in a week or so and follow up to see if more information is needed. If they ask you to resubmit, title the page, "Requested Information."

This publicity has a positive and a negative side. Many publications won't use the information until after it's stale, if at all. And they won't send you a clip for your records if they print it. On the other hand, when they print it, the value of the media does drive sales.

Clipping services can be very expensive and they won't always catch every word containing your name and book title. In addition to your own search every day, rely on friends, family, and the organizer where you're presenting. When you speak, ask the hostess for a copy of the clipping, especially when you're on the road and don't receive a daily paper. They generally have copies for you.

If you want a clipping service, maybe you're lucky enough to belong to a writing organization that has one. Those are much less costly than the major houses.

Several sources include:

- Burrelle's Information Services is an international organization. They can be contacted at 75 East Northfield Road, Livingston, New Jersey 07039, (800) 631-1160, outside the United States: (973) 992-6600. E-mail: <info@burrelles.com>

- GeoTelCorporation Newz Group has a clipping service covering seven states: Arkansas, Iowa, Kentucky, Missouri, South Carolina, West Virginia, and Texas. Contact Doug Galaska at P. O. Box 873, Columbia, MO 65205-0873, (573) 474-1111, FAX: (573) 474-1001. E-mail: <Dgalaska@newzgroup.com> or <http://www.newz.org>

- Want to get on *Oprah, Letterman, Geraldo* but not sure how to find the contact person? For the most accurate listings of the major network shows, order the *Top National TV Talk Show* spiral notebook from Bradley Communications Corporation, P. O. Box 1206, Lansdowne, PA 19050-8206. Call (800) 784-4359, ext 432. FAX: (610) 284-3704.

Can you do all this, write, and speak too? Sure you can–but do you want to? Let Chapter Six help you decide if your time and money is better spent hiring a professional

6

Whose Publicists are they anyway?

There are three types of publicists: the one the publishing house assigns to you, the one you hire out of your own pocket, and you. Can you schedule everything on your wish list, write the next novel, prepare for all the events, and have a life? You will if you have budget restraints. Hopefully, there are options.

If you were fortunate enough to be published by a large house and given an astronomical promotional budget, we're very proud for you. All you have to do is provide that person with your calendar for the oncoming year so they can schedule dates around your life. May you be blessed that they return all your calls, care about you intensely, and get you on *Oprah*. You're way ahead of the rest of us.

But, if you have a limited promotional budget from the house, or no funds at all, you'll need to define your goals early and start saving your money.

How do you find these publicists?

Do your homework.

- Your agent and the publishing house publicist are good resources.
- Seek a referral from someone who already had a major publisher with an independent publicist. Ask who they would use if they had choices.
- Look for the publicist's name on the acknowledgment page of the author you most admire in your genre.
- Ask the author, if his/her publicist isn't listed.
- At writer's conferences drop in the press room and ask their opinions.
- Check out the *Literary Market Place*.
- When the author speaks at major functions, the publicist should be there. Find him or her and introduce yourself.
- Always have your business card and your "sound byte" ready.

Before contacting a publicist, consider your needs. What do you want from your career? Do you want to be rich, famous or just move books?

- What's your goal? Make the *New York Times* best seller list?
- Increase your status with your publishing house?
- Do you need a full or part time publicist?
- Define the territory you wish to cover.
- Time constraints should coincide with pub date. Minimally, publicists need a ninety day lead time before the pub date in order to provide the highest exposure for your tour.
- What are your budget dollars?

- Research your own book tour first.
- What are the publicist's assets?
- Is this person an expert in your genre?
- Does this publicist have experience with your publishing house?
- Does he/she have contacts in the media industry, radio, television and newspapers?
- Who else does he or she represent?
- How do his or hers other clients feel about their representation?
- What is his/her physical location in proximity to you and N.Y.?
- Does he/she have the creativity and ability to make one project generate more referrals?

If you simply can't afford a publicist or want to do it entirely yourself, try the *Maximum Exposure Marketing System*. They will provide you with a loose-leaf workbook complete with fill-in-the-blank forms on all the topics you need to cover. Contact them at 888-55 TWIST, FAX: (303) 279-7950. E-mail: <twist@marketability.com>

On the other hand, if it's national publicity you seek, New York City or Los Angeles are the hubs that deliver the best results. On the west coast, one of the largest firms is *Book Publicists of Southern California*. Irwin Zucker and Barbara Gaughen-Miller's motto "Promotions in Motion" is only one minute part of their success. Barbara's *Book Blitz, Getting Your Book in the News* is a "must read" for all authors who want to sell. For information on their firm, (323) 461-3921 or FAX: (323) 461-0917.

Once you've selected a potential publicist:

- Send the publicist a galley copy, a press kit, and brief letter of introduction, asking him/her to review the material and call you for an appointment if he/she is interested.
- Type a marketing plan. Include things you'd "like" to do and places you'd like to speak. Be extravagant. The Tokyo Book Fair may be perfect for your product.
- When you first meet, take a copy of that plan.
- If there's a personality fit, and a common understanding regarding the size of the territory you wish to cover (your market focus)? Discuss fees based on your wish list. Don't faint when you hear the number. Remember you can negotiate anything, and under most circumstances you can negotiate monthly or quarterly installments.

What are your goals? Schedule another meeting when you both have had time to review the plan against each of your goals. In subsequent conversations or meetings, talk about the media territory you hope to cover with the book, and where you both agree the promotional focus should be.

What do you want him or her to do? Code each item according to whom you both agree can best schedule this event. "P" for publicist, "A" for the author, and "C" for the publishing house. This will ensure the best return for the money invested. Discuss the initial contract quote, downsizing it to fit your budget.

Can you afford it? Sign a contract with the publicist. Provide him/her with a copy of your calendar for the year ahead so he/she will not schedule conflicts disrupting your home life. Knowing that you'll be on vacation in a certain state, however, may define additional speaking engagements there.

HINT: My publicist was recommended by a mystery author I greatly admire—Taylor Smith. I sent the publicist my book and a press kit. She read it and called me. We scheduled a face-to-face meeting. I presented her with a twelve-page single-spaced wish list of everywhere I wanted to speak in 1998.

   We perused the list, selecting which items I could do best. Then, based on her assets and view of the marketplace for my product, what she could do for me. And finally, what I should expect the publishing house to do. She developed a quote and sent me a contract.

   Best promotional money I ever spent.

Talking about money, let's talk costs. The hourly rate publicists charge range from $50 to $300. Sometimes you'll get a monthly quote, also known as a monthly retainer, payable through the life of the book tour. This is usually three to four months long. Most will charge you expenses, including telephone, FAX, copies and postage. Ask for a monthly accounting.

What can you do yourself? Don't pay publicist rates for tasks that you or someone you could hire at home would do at a lower hourly rate, i.e. answer fan mail, make travel arrangements, or manage your calendar. Save the professionals for the tough stuff, like helping you sell that book.

   There'll be expenses for postage, printing, telephone and FAX. Decide how comfortable you feel, then insist on approving any singular expense above a certain dollar amount, like $50 or $100.

You can negotiate flat rates, daily rates, monthly retainers, costs plus, whatever. Remember to keep your eye on the budget dollars and define the highest result with the best publicist.

Relationships are very important. When the person is the right one for you, you'll know it. As the book tour winds down you'll feel a sense of loss for that constant contact. That's when you know you made the right decision.

In many ways, finding a publicist is like finding a literary agent. It's a marriage and like any marriage; some work, others don't. Good communication with that person, matching business styles, and being professional are imperatives. Does he or she return calls promptly and have ready answers to your questions? Is he or she accessible? Is he or she enthusiastic? What other services does your publicist offer? Does he or she offer tiered pricing? Is there a guaranteed campaign?

Looking for free publicity?

- Send your press release to Nikkie Leonard, 1368 High Site Drive, #221, Eagen, MN 55121. If you're a member of Sisters-in-Crime, she'll post it on six bulletin boards on Genie. Her online address is <NIKKIE@genie.com>

- Another place to post your tour online? Contact *Quenda Story* at 4526 Marlborough Drive, Okemos, MI 48864-2324. E-mail: <Q.STORY@genie.com>

- If you want your e-mail address listed in an online directory, send your name and e-mail address to Katherine Schniepp at <KAT.S@Genie.com>

- *M & C Marketplace Magazine* is read by more than 280,000 corporate and association meeting planners every month. For advertising information contact Maria Manaseri at Phone and FAX: (516) 757-9562.

It's almost time for your close up. Camera! Lights! Action! Let's get dressed.

7

Dress to Sell

Dress to kill—well, at least dress to sell. First impressions are everything. What are you going to wear? **Packing for the tour** shouldn't mean a fancy and costly wardrobe, but remember you represent your body of work and how you want fans to respond and remember you.

Runs in your hose or holes in your socks? Always carry a spare pair. Dress like this is a special occasion, because for you and the reader, it is. If you want the audience to remember something special about you, make it your signature.

Wear a hat when you don't get a chance to get your hair done. Keep your nails neat and attractive. That's what the fan sees when you are autographing their book.

HINT: Stan Kent writes erotic thrillers. His suits are straight from Seville Row. His hair is short and spiked with clear gel. His colorful British accent is a plus and his charm cannot be ignored. His shoes are always shined, not scuffed. He carries an extra shirt and fresh tie.

99

That spaghetti sauce isn't particularly appealing when you're the after-luncheon speaker. Club soda is a good stain remover, but not always available or effective.

Ladies, leave that charm bracelet and things that dangle and clang at home. Jewelry or other accessories should not make noise or interfere with sound quality of the microphone. They also get caught in zippers, hair, and woven material like sweaters. On radio, the earphones will mess your hair up ladies, so take a hat for later. On television, the mike is generally clipped to your shirt above the last button, or on the tie. The battery pack is looped over the waistband.

The important thing is to be honest with yourself and set the tone for what you want others to remember about you. The flight attendant will gladly take your jacket and hang it up. If the flight isn't loaded with hand-carry, you can also stow it in the overhead above your seat. If you're driving, put it on a padded hanger to reduce those sitting wrinkles.

These are items to consider packing:

- Comfortable shoes because you're going to be standing and walking a lot.
- Take a spare pair.
- A small briefcase.
- Extra business cards.
- Your value-added items like postcards.
- At least one handout should have your web site address or advertising on it.
- Several pens in the same color ink, in the event that one

is lost or runs out of ink.
- Tissue–you never know.
- Extra bookmarks or handouts that you have developed as "point-of-purchase" items.
- A note pad. Invariably someone will ask you for something you don't have, like a date to do another appearance. Jot that information down and follow it up later.

How do the professionals interview? Before going on a particular television show look for these specifics:
- Watch that format and environment of the interview. Is the program a one-on-one or panel discussion? How many minutes will your segment run?
- Will you be seated next to the host or separated by a desk or other guests? What does the backdrop look like? Who is their target audience?
- See what works and doesn't work for others.
- Pants are recommended for ladies rather than a short mini skirt. Knees are not photogenic, even for Cindy Crawford and Sharon Stone.
- Turn off the sound and watch the interaction between the host and the guest—the non-verbal things.
- What do they wear? How do they sit? What does their body language suggest?
- What are the camera angles?
- Who does the guest look at?
- Where does the moderator sit in relationship to the guest? Do you have a chair, a sofa, or a tall stool you'll have to climb up on?
- Is the guest chewing gum or playing with her hair?

- Is she adjusting a jacket that's too small or tugging at her skirt or pants? Maybe she's nervously crossing and uncrossing her legs, or worse, tapping or shaking a foot?
- Practice, practice, practice, to avoid these "tells." They distract the viewer and the host and make you a less desirable guest for a follow-up visit.
- Take the host a small gift, including your autographed book.
- Let's talk colors. White is the worst color on camera. Blue is the best. Jewel tone colors bring out the fleshy tone of your skin. Pastels wash you out. Solids are favored to patterns, but develop your own style.

Watch late night shows and see what the hosts say about what their guests are wearing. You'll be surprised if you focus on this area of the interview.

Dressing to be remembered?
If you're a Hawaiian shirt, "please look-at-me" kind of guy, then just do it. Maybe you're James Bond and like tuxedo jackets for day wear. Just do it. Don't forget, it's your style and you're entitled to set the tone for your career.

8

Your Business Plan . . .
Staying alive, staying alive

One component of your business plan is increasing your market share and sustaining sales. **How do you sustain sales when your fifteen minutes of fame has passed.** How is this done?

Lectures and speaking engagements can continue long after the tour is complete.

* Find one or more subjects that you are expert on and develop a lecture or a series.
* Tie in tapes from previous radio and/or television events to enhance the value of your product. Package them to sell.
* Network during each event with an eye toward the next appearance.
* Write a syndicated column in any publication, no matter how small. Do this for free, for the exposure. Start with one, establish a track record and extend your market into other areas.

113

- Send postcards that reach potential customers for nearly half the price of preparing and sending letter mail.
- Get testimonials and/or product endorsements. Use the ones you like to upgrade press kits, make flyers, and create ads.
- Author Gerald Schiller created a colorful coupon. For anyone who purchased an autographed copy of *The Dog That Belonged to No One*, he'd give them one dollar cash. Time sensitive to the conference, they were stuffed in tote bags and on the author's "goodie" table.
- Contact LaRee Bryant at <LBryant316@aol.com> She's the editor for *Novelist, Inc.* She's always looking for good articles relating to the professional side of writing. Don't forget to mention your work.
- Teach at a senior center, an adult education group, or start a creative writing class of your own.
- At the library, stroll through the *Literary Marketplace*, *Encyclopedia of Associations*, and *National Trade and Professional Associations*. No matter what your book is about, there's a world of book buyers waiting for you to find them. You might advertise in the newsletter or magazine, speak at trade meetings, conventions, or customize a course and offer to teach.
- Share a booth at the local trade fair.
- Who has the most popular live radio talk show? Get booked. You have something for everyone.
- Jeffrey Lant wrote *How to Earn a Whole Lot More Than a $1,000,000 a Year Writing, Selling and Commissioning How-To Information*. Read it.
- Give autographed copies of your novel to the gatekeepers (secretaries, assistants). If they read and like

it, they can help you get past that locked door.

- Find celebrity addresses who might be interested in your product and mail them copies of the book. *The Address Book* and *The Corporate Address Book* by Michael Levine has almost 10,000 listings of the famous and the infamous. Think that Reverend Billy Graham might be interested in giving you a review for your project? His address is there along with that of several convicted murderers on death row.

- *Book Page* is a monthly review that reaches hundreds of U.S. bookstores. There's an excellent opportunity, if you purchase an ad, to reach 2,500 bookstores and 3,000 libraries. Contact Julia Steele at ProMotion, Inc. 2501 21st Avenue, South #5, Nashville, TN 37212. (615) 292-8926 or (800) 726-4242. FAX: (615) 292-8249. <julia@bookpage.com> Send gallies to Carolyn Porter, the A s s i s t a n t E d i t o r at ext 11. Or to <Carolyn_Porter@bookpage.com> or Sukey Howard <sukey_howard@bookpage.com>

- Attend book fairs for your particular genre, i.e. new age, astrology, romance, western round-up days, Christian, literacy events, annual library book sales, Star Trek, nudists, whatever.

- Plan on attending the American Booksellers Association Convention, now called Book Expo.

- Attend the library convention, both regionally and national.

- Encourage other speakers or conference organizers to sell your books if you can't attend. Work out a sharing plan on the sales.

- Ask for help. "Ask" being the key word. Ask for

publicity, speaking engagements, writing opportunities, whatever you want. You will get lots of "noes" along the way. The truly successful people in this world will help others. You will pass others on your way to success.

- Is your product conducive to having a corporate or organization sponsor? That will certainly bring in more money for advertising and offer greater distribution.

Are there other ideas to consider? When speaking and selling ask yourself the following:

- Does this audience have money to purchase my book?
- Do they want my value-added products?
- Do I offer enough variety to achieve balance in those sales? How many people will attend?
- Will they buy additional copies as gifts? What is the organization about? What is its mission statement?
- Have I personalized my presentation to bond with them? Will I have all the answers to their questions? Or know where to refer them for those answers?
- Will my product solve their problems, enhance their lives, help them achieve their goals, make a positive statement?
- Is there such a great need for my product that they'll be willing to pay whatever it takes?

Once you've joined organizations and are published, work to develop co-op ads. For example, Sisters-in-Crime does two each year: One in spring and one in winter for *Publishers Weekly*. This gives you an opportunity to be seen by over 150,000 subscribers for only $40 an ad. You can't buy an advertisement at that rate in any magazine in America.

Don't forget audio and video packaging! Audio books constitute a large market of book sales. Seventy-three percent of their customer base listen to books during their long commutes to and from work. Nonfiction, entertainment, and self-help are the most popular topics. Audio Publishers Association reports that listeners select their choices based on the subject matter, then the author's reputation, and the recognition of the title. This method also helps you reach sight-impaired readers and seniors as well.

During your first year on tour, select three or four conferences to attend. Develop **value-added products.** You will complete an application and send in your registration fee. Also include your press kit, refer them to your Web site, and ask to be assigned to a panel or teach your own class. Ask the organizers if you can send tools ahead.

HINT: At the 1998 world mystery conference, I mailed post cards that showcased the book jacket and one of my book marks. Someone stuffed them into the totes that every attendee received. Out of over 250 authors there, only two had thought ahead, and I was one of them. Thirty-five hundred new fans and readers now know about my book.

Take all your promos for the "goody" table. It's usually messy and you have to stop by and straighten it up throughout the conference until they are gone; but it's worth it if you have an eye-catching item.

Hand out more promos at the door where you are speaking and take extras for the book signing table and the book sales room.

Get a blow-up of your jacket cover made into a poster. Usually a 17" x 12" will fit flat in the bottom of your luggage. Prop the poster up everywhere you are. Those cost less than five dollars each for four-color and are excellent marketing tools.

Set a goal to book a certain number of radio interviews everyday. M. Scott Peck conducted over 1,000 in his first year. Most can be taped and performed from your home, a hotel room or your mobile telephone. Those are known as "phoners." This is an example of a low budget tour.

Obtain a list of radio stations from the local libraries in cities where you know your book will be in stores. Contact the radio stations and determine if they have talk shows. Identify the producers and their guidelines for submission.

Generally a one page letter to the producer with a press kit and the twenty question and answer sheet inside is sufficient. Don't present yourself merely as an author. Focus on the fact that you're an expert about a specific topic. Hopefully you will make it timely and provocative.

Follow up with a phone call or letter. When you're booked, be certain that you're upbeat, articulate, entertaining and knowledgeable about the topic. Also, close out the world around you: the television, other telephones ringing, the children or pets. You will need total focus and be relaxed. Stress or being rushed is a death knell to your success.

Name recognition equals book sales.

The *Chicken Soup* guys say, "Get on as many magazine covers as possible."

HINT: Mid-list authors have a tougher time with this one. In 1998, for me that was July's *NEXT Magazine* cover. But three scrapbooks containing press clippings are comforting memories.

99

Ready for your close up?

To schedule your television appearances, list yourself in *Radio/TV Interview Report*. Bradley Media Publications, 135 East Plumstead Avenue, P. O. Box 1206, Lansdowne, Pennsylvania 19050-8206. (610) 259-1070. They print 35 issues a year, and will write your ad copy free and submit it to you for final approval. Since 1986, they have placed over 4,000 authors on the air. Mary Duffy, a producer for the *Montel Williams Show* says, "I love it! I use it all the time."

9

The Inner Sanctum of the Internet

The Internet has evolved technically to become the writer's best resource (dollar-for-dollar) for book reviews, interviews, book sales, and news releases. In the year 2000, it is conservatively estimated that 150,000,000 people will be on the Net. **It helps if you have a ten-year old at home who can help you** with this technology.

Customers mean readers and that translates to sales according to Netsmart Research, which says eight out of ten Internet users routinely buy products based on research online.

Today, you can conduct business on everything that touches your life. Rent an apartment, price an automobile, find a job, buy or sell stock, or bid on auction items. You can find a word in a dictionary. And locate a high school friend or a former lover. You only need to capture 15,000 of those buyers to reach the best seller list.

The explosion of modern technology would not be complete without developing its unique share of weirdos, crazies, fanatics, crooks, frauds, liars, cheats, and sickos, in addition to good folks. You'll learn words like "lurkers," "berserkers," "flaming," and "junk mail." The Internet is faceless, and anonymity sometimes breeds contempt. Like a thief in the night, one mistake and your financial, emotional, or physical life can be destroyed. Guard your assets, private numbers, and access codes. Enter this community with caution and respect.

If you're Internet impaired, find yourself a Webmaster; someone who knows how to build and maintain a site for you. **Setting up a web site** takes skill. Don't be embarrassed if these geniuses are under the age of ten.

HINT: At my first signing Raul Melendez entered my life. He built and maintains my Web site. Thank you Mel from the bottom of my life . . .

99

If you have talent, time, and the interest, develop your own. You'll need to use HTML. There are several Web writer programs, like Composer that comes with Netscape Communicator. You might download a trial copy of TUCOWS. It's easy to learn and not expensive if you decide to purchase it. Others include Claris Home Page, Microsoft Front Page, Adobe's Page Mill, and HomeSite 2.5. Because the industry is booming, please check your software stores before making a final decision.

When setting up your site, create one with its own identity. A "domain name," as it's called, is important.

- It protects your company or trademark and when others are searching for you, it makes finding you easier.
- It means you're big enough to have a domain name.
- You can switch between Internet Service Providers (ISP's) more easily.
- Make it short and sweet so it fits on your business card and is memorable.

To reserve your domain name, contact InterNIC Registration Services by calling (703) 742-4777, or e-mail them at <hostmaster@internic.net> The cost is $100 for the first year, and $50 for renewals.

Plan your page in advance. First, identify what you wish to accomplish with the site, setting goals for yourself. Next, think about a name for your URL, Uniform Resource Locator, that identifies each Web site. Make it individual so others can find you. Then design it following these ideas:

- A fast-loading graphic. For many PC owners time is money.
- A table of contents or menu bar.
- Your e-mail address as a link with a message from you to your fans.
- Links to other sites, including Amazon.com and/or Barnes&Noble.com.
- A counter may be important for the hit totals, if you're into numbers. However, the hits are there for the world to see. Would you be embarrassed if there are no hits?
- Press Releases including works in progress, appearance schedule, your bio, and photos of you and/or the book jacket cover.

- A guest book is a great way to develop an e-mail list.
- Excerpts, especially the complete first chapters, are very effective on the Net.
- Avoid huge graphics, borders, or busy backgrounds.
- Don't try fancy fonts. Go with the proven.
- Be flexible as you may change it often.

Some ISP's (Internet Service Providers) will give you a free home page if you sign up for their Internet access service. However, they may attach ads on your site, so it isn't entirely "free." Shop around before you engage someone to develop this important tool for you.

The key to the success of your site is keeping the personal message and appearance schedule current.

Is everybody else out there doing this too?

You bet! With over one million web sites, how can you garner your share of hits and buys?

- Place your site on every piece of paper that leaves your hands. Forty percent of all business cards and stationery now feature an e-mail address.
- Mention this in every presentation.
- It should be listed in all your books and placed on all flyers, brochures, or ads.
- Offer to "speak" on-line with popular zines and mention it during the "interview."
- Place it in major web directories and list it on Internet malls.
- Find special database sites and post it; i.e., if you have a bookstore, contact the ABA Bookstores at <http://www.bookweb.org/directory>.

- Cross link your site with those of the organizations you joined.
- When you're in chat rooms, mention your site.
- Do mass mailings online. PostMaster Direct at <http://www.postmasterdirect.com> has more than four million people on mailing lists.
- Rent out your own mailing list to PostMaster Direct if you have at least 5,000 names.

For more online activity whether you're interviewing, selling or wanting the book reviewed:

- If you're an expert or spokesperson for your product contact Noble Internet Directory, 25 Kearny Street, Suite 505, San Francisco, CA 94108. (800) 640-5959. E-mail <lind@noblegroup.com> They will spotlight your expertise, introduce you to speaker's bureaus and meeting planners, and promote your publications.
- Aimee Beckerman at <aimee@bookwire.com> is a book reviewer.
- Willetta Heising, with Purple Moon Press, publishes *Detecting Women Pocket Guide*. You must have two books in print to be included. But fans use this guide to collect books. Contact her at <Purplemoon@prodigy.net>.
- Mystic Ink is an online community of writers. Sunny Rhodes is the editor. Contact her at <http://www.mystic-ink.com> or <http://www.right2write.com>.
- For the latest news in trade book publishing check out <thebookreporter.com>.

- The Book Report is located at 250 E. 57th Street, Suite 1228, New York, New York 10107. They review book and conduct author interviews. Contact them at <Bookpage@aol.com>.
- <www.blackwriters.org> is the web site address for the African-American Online Writers Guild, the premier community for black writers.
- If you write poetry, check <www.borderlands.org> This is one of Texas' finest reviewers of poetry.
- If you want a copy of your favorite movie script, stop by <scriptcity.net>.
- <www.rosedog.com> is an Internet site that allows writers to showcase—free—as much work and/or biographical information as they wish. You never know when an editor, agent, or publisher will see your work and contact you. They have classified ads that include contests, writing services, consulting, workshops, conferences, reader's groups and writer's groups.
- Novel Advice is a newsletter in the AOL Writers Club devoted to the craft of writing. Try <http://www.noveladvice.com> for tips, message boards
- For those interested in Southern California, try <LITNET@BIGFOOT.COM> You'll find news about events and organizations. They have author guests and welcome on online subscribers.
- <Writersclub.com> conducts author interviews. By genre, they have chat rooms, conferences, and seminars. These are well attended.
- As an alternative to having your own web site contact Authors on the Highway, 245 W. 17th St, 5th Floor, New York, New York 10011. The FAX is (212) 337-7050.

If you send in your tour schedule, the staff will post it on their site. <Roadtrip@bookwire.com>.

- In 1993, David Knight founded BookTalk, a 24-hour recorded book discussion line. Publishers pay between $100 and $200 a month to record their authors. If the recordings stay on longer, the costs vary. The author prepares a script, does the recording and BookTalk does the taping. Hits on this line result in greater exposure and sales potential.
- Pat Holt is the former book editor for the *San Francisco Chronicle*. Her new Holt Uncensored is an online book news column, sponsored by the Northern California Independent Booksellers Association. To subscribe go to: <http://www.nciba.com/patholt.html> Her commentary includes industry issues, author interviews, book reviews and hot tips. Her e-mail address is: <holtpat@earthlink.com>.
- To reach the Canadian book market, bookstores, libraries, schools and professional groups, contact Association of Canadian Publishers, 110 Eglinton Avenue, West #401, Toronto, Ontario M4R 1A3. (416) 487-6116. FAX: (416) 487-8815. E-mail: <genny`urquhart@canbook.org> or <www.canbook.org>. This association also publishes the Directory of Canadian Media.
- To post your Canadian tour, contact Joan Nettle at Southam New Media, 44 Frid Street, Hamilton, Ontario L8N 3G3. (905) 526-2419. Or e-mail her at <jnettle@sotham.ca>.
- If your book has college level potential, don't overlook this $8.15 billion market. Thousands of college store

managers and buyers attend an annual conference. Contact the National Association of College Stores, 500 E. Lorain Street, Oberlin, OH 44074-1294. (216) 775-7777. E-mail: <info@org> or <www.nacs.org>.

- Subscribe to an Internet list for booksellers called Publishers Daily. This site contains current information and seeks blurbs on new books that will be posted.
- If your book has gossip appeal try: <www.eonline.com> Editors might feature it on *E! Online*. Doesn't hurt to try.
- The Publishers Marketing Association has an e-mail number <LISTSERV@hslc.org> They'll respond to questions you may have on marketing.
- Writing on the Edge has wonderful interviews with published writers. <EWGBet@aol.com>
- The Short Mystery Fiction Society, <majordomo@teleport.com> provides a way to see your work on screen. It's an opportunity to be discovered by other "zine" magazines. The prospects here are endless.

How do you catch the Amazon.com wave and sell your novel? Amazon began in 1995, and now boasts more than four million customers in almost two hundred countries who buy books from its website. Here are a few ideas to enhance your sales:

- You can provide Amazon with cover art, a synopsis of the work, the introduction, whatever you can to achieve the highest exposure on the net.
- There are online interviews that help introduce you to your potential audience. Reach them at

<www.amazon.com.com/authors> .

- Take advantage of developing "keywords" so your work can be associated with as many topics as possible.

- Amazon.com has many editors who will review the book. From the homepage, pull down the "subject" menu and locate the correct editor. Send that person a copy of your book to Amazon.com, 1516 Second Avenue, Seattle, WA, 98101. Include other reviews that you may have to increase the editor's interest in reviewing it for you.

- Encourage your reviewers to add their opinions to the buyers page once your book has been accepted. This generates excitement and may help the sales remain high.

- If you're self-published or from a small press with distribution concerns, talk with Amazon. They have an Advantage Program that enables them to carry a small amount of stock to assure their 24-hour shipment guarantee. They will require a discount and 55% is the recommended figure, plus free shipping. <www.amazon.com/advantage>

- If you list your Web site on the Amazon's listing, that may drive potential buyers to you. That's how you find readers and buyers interested in your product and add to your mailing list.

- If your topic is similar to a more popular book that has a huge marketing budget and publishing house, shirttail on the hits to their page. Read that book. Do a review and at the bottom, add something like "if you like this book, try . . ." And list the title of your book. People will find you who might otherwise not know you.

129

For AOL members there are many opportunities to showcase your work.

If you don't have an account call (800) 827-6364. Try the following:

• AOL Live gives its members an opportunity to showcase their products. There are chat rooms, interview shows and book reports. Take the time to learn how to participate.

• Tie your book with a special day or event using "keywords" and form a partnership to the more familiar authors and their works in this industry.

• For The Book Report, Kids Read and Book Bag forums contact Carol Fitzgerald by e-mail: <ckcf@aol.com> Her address is 250 West 57th Street, Suite 1228, New York, New York 10107. Her direct phone is (212) 246-3100. Send her copies of your book and she'll forward them to the reviewers.

You can start your own discussion group on Yahoo. Find subject matter that's related to your genre and contact staff at <http://clubs.yahoo.com>. One club will spawn another as more discussion groups interface with yours. Those are readers out there. Find them and help them find you.

You might sponsor an author chat in the World Without Borders' chat area. Check <www.wwbchat.com>. Readers have an opportunity to ask questions and receive an instant reply.

There's a bound report that shares how to getting listed on over 50 Internet book-selling sites. It's called *Sell Your Books on the Web* published by The Next Millennium. Contact editors at <visrael@nextmillen.com>.

The Internet is such a booming industry that it'd be impossible to list every possible option available to you, the author, without slighting some excellent sources. For the highest and best results on the net, review your business and marketing goals, train yourself on locating search engines that best serve your needs, and go get them.

Is your "marketing brain" kicking in? Good. Add your ideas to those in the next chapter.

10

More Marketing Mania

Every year six million manuscripts are sent to publishing houses. Of those numbers only 55,000 are accepted for publication.

If your project is nonfiction, you have a better than average opportunity to become a chosen one, because 45,000 of all manuscripts published are nonfiction.

And you only need to sell 15,000 hardback copies to become a best seller.

Did you know there are ten seasons of book selling:
- Valentine's Day
- Easter
- Mother's Day and Father's Day
- Graduation
- Summer
- Back-to-School
- Halloween
- Autumn
- Thanksgiving
- Christmas

If the genre fits any of those ten seasons, plan the marketing to enhance sales during that period of time by tie-ins to special interest groups.

- Seniors
- Baby Boomers
- Generation X's
- Children and Grandchildren
- Teenagers
- Women
- Men
- Hispanics
- African-Americans
- Businesses
- Computer and Technical
- Cooking
- Fitness
- Gardening and Home Repair
- Religious and Spiritual
- Self-help
- Travel and Leisure
- Trendy
- Poetry
- Specialty Fields like
  - Mystery
  - Sci-fi and Fantasy
  - Biography and Autobiography
  - Romance
  - Mainstream

Did you think about this? To promote your books to schools, stores, libraries and the media, associate your promotion with the more than 4,000 special days that are celebrated each year. Many of these may be obscure, but could be a great tie-in with your novel. Contact Open Horizons, P. O. Box 205, Fairfield, IA 52556-0205. (515) 472-6130 or (800) 796-6130. FAX: (515) 472-1560. E-mail: <info@bookmarket.com> or <http://www.bookmarket.com/celebrate.html> Ask for a copy of *Celebrate Today* that features over 4,300 events. Their data file contains over 10,000 events.

- Send holiday cards to all the people and organizations that you have worked with throughout the year. You want them to remember you. Not for this book; but for the next one, and the one after that.
- Send a theme card, like a birthday, Valentine Day, July 4th, to introduce your new novel. Booksellers always receive the typical things: flyers and brochures. Work outside the box and do something different.
- Adopt a charity or library and donate a specific amount; i.e., one dollar a book, or net proceeds, from the sale of each book.
- Book distributor Baker & Taylor developed a state-by-state directory of libraries that encourage author readings. Contact them at 652 E. Main Street, P. O. Box 6920, Bridgewater, New Jersey, 08807-0920. (908) 218-0400. Mary Shapiro is the editor for this directory.

HINT: After my five-part series, "So You Want to Get Published," appeared in *The Desert Woman*, a local women's newspaper, I received numerous calls from readers who read only one part and needed the others. I bound the entire series and offer it as a value-added product: three dollars when it's mailed, or two dollars as a handout.

99

- Use a money-back guarantee for books and tapes that you sell direct to the public. History indicates that the longer the guarantee, the fewer the returns.
- Make a list of all the products that can be "spun-off" your book. All the value-added items will include tapes, handouts, and goodies like T-shirts, caps, or greeting cards.
- Excerpts from your novel make great sales teasers. Type it up, bind it and give it away at selected venues.
- Many authors print the first chapter of their next book in the back of their current book. If your chapter ending hook is there, they'll want more and wait impatiently for the next one.
- In your **newsletter**, try selling ads to vendors that have a tie-in to your product.
- The Jenkins Group has formed a special sales division that helps authors and small press publishers find new markets. Contact: Nathan Tarsa at 121 East Front Street, 4th Floor, Traverse City, MI 49684. (616) 933-0445. FAX: (616) 933-0448. E-mail: <jenkinsgroup@smallpress.com> or <www.bookpublishing.com>.
- If you self-published or have a small press, don't get too discouraged about distribution. Call Ingram's title submission information hotline at (615) 287-5350, or (800) 937-8222, ext 5250. Staff will ask for four free copies of your book, plus additional documents you'll

find listed in detail at <www.ingrambook.com/Company_Info/ips>. When they've accepted your book and you want to know the inventory numbers or sales, call them and use Option 2. When you have everything in order, Contact: Sandi Wells, the supervisor in Publishers Relations Department Distribution Group, One Ingram Boulevard, LaVergne, TN 37086-3629. (615) 287-5369 or (800) 937-8222, ext 5369. FAX: (615) 287-5430. E-mail: <sandi.wells@ingrambook.com> or <www.ingrambook.com> Others in her department include Joanne Gay, ext 5382 and Erica Littles, ext. 5380.

- **Sell on television.** QVC and Home Shopping Network sell books. They are particularly interested in theme books. Contact their producer and get a list of future programming themes. Make it work for you.

- QVC Network is located at 1365 Enterprise Drive, Westchester, PA 19380, (215) 430-1000, FAX: (215) 430-1052.

- Home Shopping Network is at 1 HSN Drive, St. Petersbury, FL 33729, (813) 572-8585.

- Create your own **newsletter** that keeps your reader in your writing and touring life. Many authors have a newsletter instead of a web site. Others have both.

- *Brands and Their Companies, A Gale Trade Names Directory* is an excellent resource for promotional tie-ins for your novel. Contact Gale Research, Inc. at 835 Penobscot Building, 645 Griswold Street, Detroit, MI 48226-4094, (313) 961-2242 or (800) 877-4253, FAX: (313) 961-6083. Home Page: <www.gale.com>.

137

- If your genre might interest the law enforcement community, contact Calibre Press at 666 Dundee Road, #1607, Northbrook, Ill 60062-2760 or (847) 498-5680. E-mail: <Staff@calibrepress.com> or <www.calibrepress.com> They publish *Street Survival Newsline*, a twice-weekly e-mail newsletter that reaches 600,000 law enforcement professionals in the United States. Their subscribers print out the "ezine," share it with other officers, post it on bulletin boards at the station, and often quote from them in other meetings. The publisher claims an additional 250,000 readership from this broadcasting approach.

- Major hotel chain Holiday Inn has a magazine *NAVIGATOR* which is a prime place to promote your book. Contact Susan Rodell at 1301 Carolina Street, Greensboro, North Carolina 27401. E-mail <surodell@aol.com>.

- Does your product include sharp tips, clever strategies, make readers feel better? Try the *Bottom Line/Personal* newsletter. With 1.5 million readers don't overlook this market. Contact Boardroom, Inc. 55 Railroad Avenue, Greenwich, CT, 06836-2614. (203) 625-5900. FAX: (203) 861-7443. Home Page: <http://www.Broadroom.com> or <webteam@boardroom.com> They'll direct you to the department that matches your message.

- Buy a coupon ad in the advertising section of your Yellow Pages.

- Ask for a seat toward the front of the plane and get on early. Your book or other promotional items should be visible. Have extras to give away.

HINT: My book marks are in high demand. I often hand them out at airports, on airplanes, and in public places all over the world. People see them and make a comment. I give them one indicating I've written a book and if they like mysteries, they might think about ordering a copy. It helps tremendously when my hubby says, "My wife's the author. It's a really good read."

- Buy a coupon ad in any newsletter or magazine if you have a tie-in item. It your book is about flying, contact airline magazines, the travel agency association and your personal agent.
- Book distributor Baker & Taylor and White Bridge Communications (a subsidiary of Ingram) both publish winter holiday catalogs. They may be expensive, but they reach more than 500,000 book buyers. Baker & Taylor is located at 652 East Main Street, P. O. Box 734, Bridgewater, New Jersey, 08807, (908) 722-8000, FAX: (908) 722-0184. White Bridge Communications, Inc. is located at 1136 Heil Quaker Blvd, La Vergne, TN 37086, (615) 287-5628, FAX: (615) 287-5644. E-mail: <nancy.wise@ingrambook.com>.
- Create "continuous loop" videotape of reviews and promos for trade shows and bookstores.
- Are you sick? Know someone who is? Distribute

"waiting room" copies all the way to the cemetery. And there too, if your product is a natural tie-in.

- *Chicken Soup, Dummies, Goosebumps, Kiplinger*, and *One Minute Manager* are examples of brand name success stories. Add your own to this impressive list.
- If you're promoting a cause, co-op with them for sales if they distribute and/or advertise your product.
- Free, local newspapers and publications are found in news stands or restaurants throughout your community. They are additional sources for interviews with you and about your book.
- Create that market by having someone read your book and do a review.
- Local "throw-away" papers need filler articles, especially when they don't have to pay a reporter for it. Both you and the publisher have a win-win here.
- Write an article or series of articles. At the end of each article add something like, ". . . is the author of . . ." Never overlook an opportunity to write down the title of your current work.
- Never miss an opportunity to "say" the name of your book.
- The Lifestyle editor of your local paper may be more interested in you and your book than the book review editor. Your book is an extension of you. You are an inspiration to readers and, hopefully, you are the expert on your subject.
- Libraries usually honor requests from their patrons. Have your friends and family drop notes in the suggestion boxes requesting your book.

HINT: One local library had two copies of my book and developed a long waiting list. Someone rented one copy and refused to return it, paying the library full price for it. The librarian called and ordered several more books.

- If you own a retail store or restaurant, or have friends who do, set up a "business card fish bowl" and offer a book as a weekly or monthly drawing. This is an excellent way to build up your mailing list.
- Never overlook an opportunity to barter. It's still big business.
- Scott Flanders, president of Macmillan Computer Publishing has been quoted, "We say that there are two successful books on the subject: The first one out and the best one." In your case, try to be both.
- Price your seminar and workshops to include copies of the book for each attendee.

Publishers Weekly plans issues well in advance and, as you may know, focuses on specific concepts. One week may be children, another religion, yet another romance or mystery. Check PW's site at <www.publishersweekly.com> to determine what the upcoming issues will cover. If you have an idea for an article or want to pitch a story, contact them at 245 West 17th Street, New York, New York 10011. (212) 645-0067. FAX: (212) 463-6631.

Probably one of the boldest and most successful marketing coups of 1999 belongs to mystery author Lisa Scottoline. She posted a draft version of her first chapter to her

Web site, then invited the "hits" to try their hands editing it.

The press, including *The Wall Street Journal* and *The New York Times,* picked it up, which prompted hundreds more "wanna be" editors to log on her site.

It'd be interesting to know, in the end, how many "editors" plunked down the $20 to buy her hardback to see if their edits were taken to heart. Way to go!

If you find something that really works for you—keep doing it again and again. You may re-write, re-title, or develop a new idea for distributing the product. Just do it. Set yourself a marketing goal each day to take action, even if it's just writing a letter, making a few calls, or doing one radio interview. It doesn't take time; it takes effort. But it's worth all this to keep your book alive for years.

"

So, there you have it. I've shared my victories and my stories with you. Life is a learning experience. And learning is a daily event. If you have any clever marketing ideas that you'd like to share with others, please write me. If you tried something and fell flat on your face, tell me that story too. We all need humor in our lives.

The road to publication is riddled with rejection. The path to sales, marketing and promotion is a mystical puzzle. I believe the gift of sharing is very important. That's why I wrote this book. Who knows? You and your book title may be among those quoted in the next edition of this book.

Did you read the paragraphs above? I just gave you a shameless opportunity to promote yourself and your book in my next edition—for free! Have you learned anything about promoting and marketing yet? So power up your life and let me hear from you.

Index

146

Not all references to certain words have been included in the Index. Words, such as "fax," "E-Mail," "Web site," etc., form part of addresses and in those instances have been omitted from the Index.

POWER Marketing
YOUR NOVEL

It's easy to obtain additional copies of this book for you, or your organization. Just send the Order Form from the next page with your Check, or Money Order to our Special Order Department.

All prices include shipping!

 1 copy of "Power Marketing" @ $13.00 = **$13.00**
 2 copies of "Power Marketing" @ $12.50 = **$25.00**
 3 copies of "Power Marketing" @ $12.25 = **$36.75**
 4 copies of "Power Marketing" @ $12.00 = **$48.00**
 5 copies of "Power Marketing" @ $11.50 = **$57.50**
 6 copies of "Power Marketing" @ $11.00 = **$66.00**
 7 copies of "Power Marketing" @ $10.50 = **$73.50**
 8 copies of "Power Marketing" @ $10.00 = **$80.00**
 9 copies of "Power Marketing" @ $ 9.50 = **$85.50**
10 copies of "Power Marketing", or more: **$ 9.00 each**

Wholesale prices (established book stores, or libraries only) are available upon request from Intercontinental Publishing, P.O. Box 7242, Fairfax Station, VA 22039.

For a complete list of books published by Intercontinental Publishing, please write to P.O. Box 7242, Fairfax Station, VA 22039, or call (703) 369-4992; FAX: (703) 670-7825.

Special Order Form

To:
Intercontinental Publishing
Dept PMB 208
50855 Washington Street, #C
La Quinta, CA 92253

Please ship _____ Copies of "Power Marketing Your Novel"

@ $ _____ each for a total of $ _____

My check, or Money Order is enclosed.(U.S. Funds only) and
I understand that this price <u>includes all shipping and handling</u>.

Send books to:

Name: _____

Address: _____

City: _____ State: _____ ZIP: _____

Books will be shipped via USPS (Book Rate), or via USPS Priority Mail, at
the option of the Publisher. For overnight delivery, add $7.50 per order.

The Cop Was White As Snow

Joyce Spizer

THE COP'S SUICIDE on a lonely beach confirmed his guilt. He had been skimming cocaine from police impounds and selling it to drug dealers to support his own habit and a growing taste for luxury. But he was Mel's Dad, and she was not about to accept this for a minute. Her Dad was no dirty cop!

THE COP WAS WHITE AS SNOW is a fast read. Spizer does a good job of keeping the action coming. Her insight as an investigator resonates throughout the book.
   —Barbara Seranell, author of No Human Involved

JOYCE SPIZER is the shamus she writes about. The novels in the Harbour Pointe Mystery Series are fictionalized accounts of cases she has investigated. A member of Sisters in Crime, she hobnobs regularly with other mystery writers. She lives in Southern California with her husband and co-investigator, Harold.

SBN 1-886411-83-7
LCCN: 97-39430
$10.95